TECHNICAL REPORT MARCH 2018

Organizing Early Education for Improvement

Testing a New Survey Tool

Stacy B. Ehrlich, Debra M. Pacchiano, Amanda G. Stein, and Maureen R. Wagner
with Stuart Luppescu, Sangyoon Park, Elizabeth Frank, Holly Lewandowski, and Christopher Young

TABLE OF CONTENTS

1 Introduction

Chapter 1
5 Quantitative Validation Study

Chapter 2
30 Qualitative Validation Study

Chapter 3
42 Discussion and Implications

48 References

53 Appendix

Cite as: Ehrlich, S.B., Pacchiano, D.M., Stein, A.G., Wagner, M.R., Luppescu, S., Park, S., Frank, E., Lewandowski, H., & Young, C. (2018). *Organizing early education for improvement: Testing a new survey tool*. Chicago, IL: University of Chicago Consortium on School Research and the Ounce of Prevention Fund.

Introduction

Decades of evidence demonstrates that high-quality, well-implemented early childhood education (ECE) can positively impact the learning trajectories of low-income or otherwise vulnerable children who are likely to start school with lower skills than their more advantaged peers. Yet, studies indicate that ECE programs nationwide struggle with implementing high-quality programming. As a consequence, they fall short of advancing children's learning enough to narrow achievement gaps that are already evident by the time children enter kindergarten.

Despite years of professional development efforts and investments to improve preschool classrooms, research confirms that instructional quality remains mediocre. The majority of observed classroom interactions—a key measure of instructional quality—rate well below the level associated with promoting children's academic and social gains.[1] Lower instructional quality is disproportionally found in classrooms serving low-income or otherwise at-risk children who stand to benefit the most from high-quality early childhood programming.[2] Overall, the pace and level of impact of ECE improvement efforts have been underwhelming.

When defining quality and investing in improvement, the ECE field has the potential to broaden what it considers as key levers for positive change—in particular, the organizational climate and conditions that surround teachers and teaching to enable effective daily practice. We know that schools and community-based ECE programs are complex organizations; what occurs in the classroom is influenced by the policies, practices, and relationships across the entire organization. In fact, growing research evidence from K-12 education highlights the importance of "organizational climate and conditions" for improving school performance.[3] Furthermore, research focused on particular organizational aspects of ECE programs—such as strong leadership or trusting working environments—

---

1 Aikens, Klein, Tarullo, & West (2013); Burchinal, Vandergrift, Pianta, & Mashburn (2010); Office of Head Start, Administration for Children & Families (2013, 2014, 2015).
2 Valentino (2017).
3 e.g., Allensworth, Ponisciak, & Mazzeo (2009); Bryk, Sebring, Allensworth, Luppescu, & Easton (2010); Kraft, Marinell, & Shen-Wei Yee (2016); Kraft & Papay (2014); Pallas & Buckley (2012).

suggests that programs with supportive culture and climate are also more likely to exhibit higher instructional quality.[4]

With the intention of raising the performance of programs, the ECE field has made substantial investments targeted at improving what occurs within the classroom itself (including structures, such as materials and schedule, curriculum, and interactions among teachers and students). To supplement this, reliable and valid tools exist to measure classroom structural quality, classroom interactions and instruction, interactions with families, and administrative practices.[5] However, these existing tools do not capture information on the complex, interdependent, organizational conditions that either support or impede educators' practices on a daily basis.[6] The ECE field is missing a statistically valid tool that measures these organizational conditions in ECE settings and provides actionable information from which to design improvement strategies. Without a simultaneous focus on strengthening both classroom practices *and* the organizational contexts that enable effective implementation, it is unlikely the field will realize full returns on its investments to improve the quality of ECE.[7]

Accordingly, the Ounce of Prevention Fund (Ounce) and the University of Chicago Consortium on School Research (UChicago Consortium) have partnered to develop and test the *Early Education Essential Organizational Supports* measurement system (*Early Ed Essentials*[8]), a set of teacher and parent surveys designed to measure the organizational supports of school and center-based ECE settings. The ultimate purpose of the *Early Ed Essentials* measurement system is to provide reliable and valid survey data to help programs diagnose strengths and weaknesses in their organizational conditions. By providing data and feedback, these surveys could then be used by program staff to strengthen the conditions that enable more effective teaching and thus improvements in children's learning in early education programs. Toward that purpose, we made intentional efforts to ensure our survey development methods were highly rigorous, and we attended to deep knowledge of early childhood education and programs to ensure the survey constructs were sensitive to those nuanced structures and practices. Additionally, the *Early Ed Essentials* are designed to measure key organizational constructs that will broaden the ECE field's understanding of "high-quality" programming and indicate related policy levers to inform quality improvement strategies at multiple levels.

The *Early Ed Essentials* is based on the five essentials framework, developed by Tony Bryk and colleagues.[9] This framework identifies five organizational features of schools that interact with life inside classrooms and are essential to growth in student achievement: Effective Leadership, Collaborative Teachers, Involved Families, Supportive Environment, and Ambitious Instruction.[10] Longitudinal research conducted by the UChicago Consortium indicated that teacher and student surveys measuring these five essential supports strongly predicted which schools were most and least likely to show improvement in student engagement and achievement over time.[11] Elementary schools strong in three or more of these essential supports were 10 times more likely than schools weak in most supports to substantially improve student achievement in reading and math. Research in

---

[4] e.g., Burchinal et al. (2010); Dennis & O'Connor (2013); Rohacek, Adams, Kisker, Danziger, Derrick-Mills, & Johnson (2010); Whalen, Horsley, Parkinson, & Pacchiano (2016).
[5] Bryant (2010).
[6] Zaslow, Tout, & Martinez-Beck (2010).
[7] Fixsen, Naoom, Blase, & Friedman, R. M. (2005); Whalen et al. (2016).
[8] These have formerly been called the *Five Essentials-Early Education* measurement system or surveys. We have revised the name to reflect the ongoing learning about the key organizational constructs that can be measured by surveys in ECE settings and to allow for ongoing testing of the factor structure of measures comprising these surveys over time and with more data.
[9] Bryk et al. (2010).
[10] The original five essentials were called school leadership, professional capacity, parent-community-school ties, student-centered learning environment, and instructional guidance (Bryk et al., 2010). The titles were changed in recent years when UChicago Impact began administering surveys and providing reports to individual schools.
[11] Bryk et al. (2010).

early education settings likewise indicates that programs more successfully promote children's learning and development when there are organizational structures in place to support a positive professional climate and educator's continuous learning and improvement.[12]

From 2014-16, our team engaged in a rigorous and iterative development and testing process to adapt the K-12 *5Essentials* teacher survey for applicability in ECE and created a new ECE parent survey. In a prior publication, we described that survey development and testing process, highlighting the applicability of the essential support constructs and the importance of these new surveys to the ECE field.[13] In this report, we share findings from the next stage of our survey development work—a validation study to test if the adapted and new surveys are reliable, function well across ECE settings, and are concurrently valid.

The goal of this validation study was to determine if the newly adapted *Early Ed Essentials* teacher and parent surveys capture credible and useful information about the organizational conditions of ECE settings. Specifically, we examined whether the results of the surveys aligned with other existing indicators of high-quality programming for each site. Before our surveys reach the field for use broadly, we want to be confident our surveys are sensitive enough to measure aspects of early education settings to which early childhood education leaders, practitioners, and stakeholders are attuned. This report also uses the descriptions and experiences of ECE leaders, teachers, and families to offer a window into what the organizational essential supports looked like in ECE programs and the characteristics most differentiating sites with high and low *Early Ed Essentials* survey scores.

To address these goals, our validation study and this report answer the following questions:

1. **Are the *Early Ed Essentials* teacher and parent surveys psychometrically sound?**
   In particular, we asked whether 1) survey measures (or scales) reliably assess the perceptions and experiences of the people who answer the survey items (internal validity); 2) survey items are interpreted in similar ways by people in different groups—for example, those who respond about a community-based ECE site or a school-based ECE site or those who take the parent survey in different languages; and 3) survey measures are sensitive enough to measure differences across ECE sites [sensitivity].

2. **Are responses to the *Early Ed Essentials* surveys positively related to desirable outcomes in early education programs?**
   To answer this question, we examined whether site-level survey responses are related to observed teacher-child interactions (CLASS Pre-K) and student outcomes (attendance) at those ECE sites [concurrent validity]. If the surveys are measuring organizational constructs that research suggests are important for practitioners, parents, and program support organizations to attend to, then survey results should be related to established measures of ECE quality. On the other hand, we do not expect the survey data to map perfectly onto these other measures—they should be providing consistent information while also identifying practices and experiences that other tools do not yet capture.

3. **Are there qualitatively different climate, structures, and practices between ECE sites with high vs. low *Early Ed Essentials* survey scores?**
   This question explored whether there is evidence of discriminant validity—in other words, whether the surveys are able to distinguish between programs with qualitatively different climate and culture. When survey responses indicate weak organizational supports in some sites and strong organizational support

---

12 Dennis & O'Connor (2013); Whalen et al. (2016).
13 Ehrlich, Pacchiano, Stein, & Luppescu (2016).

in others, are those differences also discernable through observation and discussions with leaders, staff, and families of those respective sites? This, in a sense, provides "practical" validation for what the surveys are measuring. The final chapter of this report provides qualitative descriptions of the differences in practices and experiences of staff and families in strong and weak sites.

Over the course of the 2015-16 school year, we conducted research to answer these questions that included both quantitative and qualitative data collection and analyses. We begin by presenting our quantitative methods and findings, which address our first two research questions about the measurement functionality and validity of the *Early Ed Essentials* surveys. Next, we present our qualitative methods and findings, which address our third research question about the discriminate validity of the surveys. Finally, we offer reflections on the implications of these findings for policy, practice, and research and describe future directions of our work. Overall, the goal of this report is to provide results addressing the research questions above, to offer evidence of the technical adequacy of the *Early Ed Essentials* surveys, and to articulate potential implications for ECE stakeholders. This report will equip ECE decision-makers with necessary information about which constructs the *Early Ed Essentials* surveys do and do not measure and how well they measure those constructs.

CHAPTER 1
Quantitative Validation Study

During 2015-16, the UChicago Consortium and the Ounce collected *Early Ed Essentials* survey data from teachers and parents and obtained student- and classroom-level outcome data in a sample of ECE sites in Chicago. In this chapter, we describe our methods and findings around survey measure development, defining each of our essentials, and relating the surveys to outcomes. This last step—assessing concurrent validity—helps us understand if there are relationships between constructs being measured by the surveys and other metrics of quality of ECE programs. These relationships will be examined at the site level, meaning that we are aggregating survey responses and outcomes to the school or center level for analyses.

Quantitative Validation Study Design

Sample

The *Early Ed Essentials* surveys were developed for use by part- or full-day, publicly-funded (e.g., state-funded preschool, Head Start) early education programs serving preschool children in either school- or community-based settings.[14] Our validation sample, therefore, excluded child care and preschool programs that did *not* receive public funding supporting early education.[15] School-based sites included different pre-kindergarten (pre-k) program models and funding streams, such as Head Start, Preschool for All (Illinois's state-funded program), Child-Parent Centers,[16] and Montessori. All community-based sites were Head Start programs, although they may have also blended funding streams and program models.

Eligible programs had at least three classrooms and, therefore, at least six educators. We chose this as a minimum requirement for both theoretical and statistical reasons. First, these surveys are intended to measure the *organizational structures* that support educators to be effective in their work with children and families. To be considered an organization, programs must be large enough to enable structures allowing for leaders who support the work of staff across multiple classrooms.[17] Second, we included programs large enough to provide ample data per site to reduce uncertainty in our survey measure estimates and allow for anonymity in responses.

Eligible programs for inclusion in our study were, therefore, school-based and community-based programs (henceforth called "sites") with three or more pre-k classrooms (serving three- and/or four-year-olds) and at least six teachers (leads or assistants) located in Chicago, IL. To select our sample from the full population of eligible sites, we used a stratified sampling method by applying PROC SURVEYSELECT in SAS, which selected a random

---

14 Similarly to other researchers, we define early childhood education programs as those "designed to enhance academic skills and behaviors of preschoolers prior to entry to school" (Howes et al., 2008, p. 27).
15 In addition, programs that only received public funding in the form of child care subsidy or block grant funding are not included in our study.
16 For more information see http://www.cps.edu/Schools/EarlyChildhood/Pages/Childparentcenter.aspx
17 We consider a program with three classrooms to be the smallest version of an "organization." In these cases, there are at least six teachers and someone who plays the role of a director. We hypothesize that the interactions and supports necessary in this scenario are similar to those in larger organizations. Future research, however, will be needed to disentangle questions of organization size and how that relates to the *Early Ed Essentials*.

sample of each strata (or group). We stratified based on the percent of pre-k students who spoke Spanish.[18] Post-selection, we visually confirmed that site locations were varied across the city of Chicago. After receiving approval from governing agencies—Chicago Public Schools (CPS) for school-based sites and the City of Chicago Department of Family & Support Services (DFSS) for community-based Head Start sites[19]—research team members contacted site leadership (principals or directors) for permission to include them in this study. In doing so, these leaders agreed to allow us to obtain administrative data about their site (from their governing agencies) and collect survey data at their site. Of the sites selected and contacted for recruitment (n=146), 55 percent agreed to participate. Participation rates were 57 percent and 54 percent for school- and community-based settings, respectively, resulting in a final sample of 81 sites—41 school-based and 40 community-based.

Sixty-five sites (31 school-based, 34 community-based) were selected and contacted, but not included in the study. Of these, 36 (15 school-based, 21 community-based) declined participation, 17 (15 school-based, 2 community-based) were unresponsive, and 12 (1 school-based, 11 community-based) were excluded due to having fewer than three pre-k classrooms. Participation rates were higher among majority-Latino sites (59 percent) than among majority-Black sites (51 percent).

Table 1 displays the average characteristics of sites in our sample; thus, these are averages of site-level averages. An "average" site in our validation study served 109 students, who lived in neighborhoods that were relatively poorer than other Chicago neighborhoods. (**See "Student Background Administrative Data"** section for calculation of average concentration of neighborhood poverty and average neighborhood educational and professional attainment). The majority of these students were three- or four-year-old Black or Latino children. On average in the sample sites, about 15 percent had been identified as students with disabilities and about 40 percent of students did not speak English as their first language.[20] Compared to CPS schools across the district and community-based programs across DFSS, our study sample had an over-representation of Latino students and under-representation of Black students. However, the rate of non-English speakers was comparable to that of the state of Illinois.[21] For school-based sites, on average, our sample sites served less-impoverished students (average standardized concentration of neighborhood poverty of 0.26 vs. 0.36 across all schools[22]). For both school- and community-based sites, the average percent of students with disabilities served was comparable to sites across the population.

---

18   Because language and race/ethnicity are highly correlated, it was unnecessary to also stratify based on race/ethnicity.
19   All programs fell under the auspices of either the City of Chicago Department of Family & Support Services (DFSS) or Chicago Public Schools (CPS).
20   Park, O'Toole, & Katsiaficas (2017). Comparatively, nearly 42 percent of three- and four-year-olds in pre-k nationally are dual language learners.
21   Barnett et al. (2016); Park et al. (2017).
22   We did not have individual-level data for all children enrolled in DFSS sites, so we could not calculate the population-level comparison for them.

TABLE 1
Average Site-level Characteristics of Validation Study Sample

	Mean	Standard Deviation
Number of Students	109	64
Percent Male	52%	7 pp[b]
Percent 2-Year-Olds	8%	9 pp
Percent 3-Year-Olds	41%	7 pp
Percent 4-Year-Olds	51%	11 pp
Percent White	6%	14 pp
Percent Black	38%	41 pp
Percent Latino	51%	39 pp
Percent Asian	2%	7 pp
Percent Other Ethnicity	2%	3 pp
Percent Non-English Native Speaker	38%	32 pp
Percent Special Education	13%	12 pp
Average Neighborhood Concentration of Poverty[a]	0.38	0.57
Average Neighborhood Educational and Professional Attainment[a]	-0.52	0.61

Note: [a] Calculated based on census information about the census block on which each student lives. All neighborhoods across Chicago were standardized, such that 0 represents the average neighborhood in Chicago and a change of +/- 1 represents a neighborhood above/below the average by one standard deviation. See student background administrative data for full description.

[b] pp = Percentage point

Survey Data Collection Procedures

Survey data collection occurred during the spring of the 2015-16 school year. In CPS elementary schools, teacher surveys were available to all staff from January 11 to March 11. After the close of this districtwide survey window, we made an alternative (but identical) version of the survey available through Qualtrics to schools in our validation study whose teacher response rate did not meet the minimum threshold. This alternate survey was open from April 25 to July 1. Parent surveys were collected in schools using Qualtrics, between February 3 and June 20. In community-based centers, research team members collected both parent and teacher surveys on-site between February 16 and July 6.

Teacher Surveys

Teacher surveys were available online in English. In school-based sites, staff survey responses were collected as part of the annual *5Essentials* survey administered online to school-based staff throughout Chicago.[23] In community-based sites, staff survey responses were collected on-site by data collectors using electronic tablets. Teachers who were not able to complete the survey at the time of on-site data collection were given a link to the survey to complete online at their convenience.

We aimed to collect survey responses from least 50 percent of all pre-k staff (teachers and teaching assistants) or at least six individuals, whichever number was greater. We sought at least six responses to protect anonymity and to decrease, as best we could, the imprecision of site-level survey measure scores.[24] For sites that were large enough, a 50 percent response rate was the determined threshold, in order to ensure representativeness of responses. For sites with teacher participation rates below this target, reminder emails were sent to the site directors and/or teaching staff. All sites that reached their target for teacher survey participation received children's books worth approximately $50.

---

23 The district (CPS) uses the *5Essentials* survey (K-12 version) annually for staff of all grade levels. The *Early Ed Essentials* specific questions were included in the survey for the 2015-16 academic year for pre-k staff.

24 Power analyses conducted determined that this is enough responses to detect differences across sites. To obtain the desired power of 0.80, we required a balance between minimum number of educator/parent responses per program and minimum number of programs. Using Optimal Design (OD) software (Liu, Spybrook, Congdon, Martinez, & Raudenbush, 2005), we calculated that with a minimum of six educators or parents per program, a medium effect size of 0.40, ρ=0.15 (based on intraclass correlations (ICCs) typically seen on our *5Essentials* K-8 teacher measures), and an α=0.05, we would need a minimum of 60 programs. To calculate necessary sample size to achieve power, one necessary parameter is the effect size. In the present analyses, we are not measuring the impact of an intervention on outcomes, but rather estimating program-level measures. We chose to use a medium effect size of 0.40, which seems reasonable given that the difference in scores between a top-scoring and bottom-scoring teacher on one of the existing *5Essentials* K-8 teacher measures is 1.3 standard deviations. All this considered, given that we had 81 sites with surveys, we met all criteria of the power analyses with at least six respondents per site. In addition, we expected to have greater precision than these assumptions. Our 3-level HLMs will nest person measurement error (L1) within educators/parents (L2) within program (L3), increasing precision.

Parent Surveys

Parent surveys were available online and in paper form, in both English and Spanish. Parent survey data collection was conducted by research team members on-site at both school- and community-based sites. Participation was voluntary; flyers explaining the purpose of the survey and details of data collection were distributed by staff at the sites to parents prior to data collection. Parents were approached during drop-off and/or pick-up by research staff and invited to complete the online survey using electronic tablets. Paper surveys were available for parents who preferred paper copies, when there were more parents than tablets available, or for rare occasions when tablets were unable to connect to the internet. In limited cases where parents were unable to read and complete the survey independently (e.g., due to barriers of sight or literacy), data collectors provided an accommodation by reading the questions to the parent and recording responses.

Our target was to collect survey responses from parents of at least 25 percent, and no more than 50 percent, of the total number of preschool-age students enrolled at a site, as reported by the program or school. The maximum was determined based on limitations of funding for incentives. Parent surveys were administered until the 25 percent target was met. As such, for certain sites, data was only collected at drop-off or for parents with children in a morning half-day session or afternoon half-day session. Data collection was scheduled in coordination with the site, and considered convenience for parents and staff members, likelihood of meeting the target, and other considerations or logistics raised by the site coordinator. If the target for parent surveys was not reached in one day, more dates were scheduled to administer the rest of the surveys. Each respondent received a $5 gift card.

Teacher and Parent Survey Data

Overall, 746 teacher surveys and 2,464 parent surveys were collected between winter and spring 2016. **Table 2** shows the breakdown of survey data collected by the type of ECE site. For the parent survey, which was offered both online and via paper-pencil, the majority (72 percent) were completed online using electronic tablets. Two-thirds of parent surveys were completed in English in both school-based and community-based sites. Across all sites, an average of 75 percent of teachers responded to the survey (79 percent in school-based and 71 percent in community-based) and 31 percent of parents responded to the survey (32 percent in school-based and 31 percent in community-based).

TABLE 2

Survey Data Collection Completion Rates

	School-Based Sites	Community-Based Sites	Total
Total Number of Surveys Completed (Response Rate)			
Teacher Surveys	451 (79%)	294 (71%)	745 (75%)
Parent Surveys	1,463 (32%)	1,001 (31%)	2,464 (31%)
Breakdown of Parent Survey Language and Modality (% within Language/Modality, by Agency)			
Language			
# English Parent Surveys	963 (65.8%)	668 (66.7%)	1631 (66.2%)
# Spanish Parent Surveys	500 (34.2%)	333 (33.3%)	833 (33.8%)
Modality			
# Online Surveys	1016 (69.4%)	775 (77.4%)	1791 (72.7%)
# Paper-Pencil Surveys	447 (30.6%)	226 (22.6%)	673 (27.3%)
Number of Sites Meeting Data Collection Thresholds			
Teacher Survey (either value of 6 or 50%, whichever is greater)	37 of 41 (90.2%)	32 of 40 (80.0%)	69 of 81 (85.2%)
Parent Survey (25% or greater)	38 of 41 (92.7%)	39 of 40 (97.5%)	77 of 81 (95.1%)

Based on the criteria described under the "**Survey Data Collection Procedures**" section, about 85 percent of sites met the teacher survey criteria. More school-based sites met the minimum of six staff members or 50 percent (whichever was greater) than community-based sites. Parent survey criteria was met in 95 percent of sites. As described in the "**Analysis**" section, we conducted analyses on all data available with additional sensitivity checks by reducing our sample to those who met these criteria.

Measures

Surveys

The original version of the *Early Ed Essentials* teacher survey used in this validation study included 26 measures and 164 items. On average, the teacher surveys took about 35–40 minutes to complete in center-based sites; since school-based teachers took the survey through the larger district-wide administration of the *5Essentials* surveys, we do not know how long individual survey completion took. The original version of the *Early Ed Essentials* parent survey included 9 measures and 54 items. On average, the surveys took parents 15-20 minutes to complete.

Student Background Administrative Data

Administrative data were made available to the research team through data sharing agreements with two agencies—CPS for school-based sites and DFSS for community-based Head Start sites. Data included background characteristics for all preschool students enrolled in participating sites including: race/ethnicity, gender, date of birth, special education status, home language, address, and the site at which they were enrolled. Using the home address, we created variables from the 2012 American Community Survey at the census block level that represented students' average neighborhood concentration of poverty and average neighborhood educational and professional attainment. Average neighborhood concentration of poverty is calculated as a composite made from the male unemployment rate and the percentages of families under the poverty line. Average neighborhood educational and professional attainment is a composite made from the mean level of education of adults and the percentage of employed persons who work as managers or professionals. Both were standardized across neighborhoods with a mean of 0 and a standard deviation of 1. These variables were used as covariates in our analytic models.

Outcome Measures

Outcome data were also obtained directly from CPS or DFSS. Site-level outcomes were explored using two metrics: 1) classroom observations of teacher-child interactions using the Classroom Assessment Scoring System (CLASS) Pre-K[25], and 2) student attendance.[26]

CLASS Pre-K. The CLASS is an observation tool that measures the quality of teacher-child interactions in preschool classrooms in the domains of Emotional Support, Classroom Organization, and Instructional Support. Research shows that children in preschool classrooms with higher CLASS scores are better prepared for kindergarten,[27] and children who enter kindergarten with stronger readiness skills attain higher achievement scores through tenth grade.[28] The CLASS is widely used to measure improvement in early education; it has been incorporated into the federal monitoring and compliance review process for Head Start grantees and, more recently, into some state accountability systems, which historically focused only on structural elements of quality.[29]

CLASS data were provided directly from CPS and DFSS.[30] Within each agency, observations were conducted by external data collectors who had participated in rigorous observer reliability training, with certification reassessed on an annual basis. When the language of instruction was a language other than English, bilingual data collectors observed in those classrooms. Our data included CLASS scores for classrooms across 37 school-based sites (120 classrooms) and 40 community-based sites (150 classrooms), with an average of 3.5 classrooms per site. Overall, classrooms in our sample had an average score of 6.13 on Emotional Support (SD = 0.69), 5.99 on Classroom Organization (SD = 0.97), and 3.16 on Instructional Support (SD = 1.16). The lower scores and wider spread on Instructional Support is consistent with nationwide patterns.[31] A similar pattern was observed when we examined model-fitted CLASS scores at the site-level:[32] Sites had average scores of 6.18 on Emotional Support (SD = 0.42), 6.06 on Classroom Organization (SD = 0.66), and 3.25 on Instructional Support (SD = 0.65).[33] The intra-class correlation for each domain was 0.507, 0.577, and 0.445, respectively. **Figure 1** shows how CLASS scores were distributed across 77 sites with data. We aimed to have CLASS scores for at least three classrooms, or 50 percent of classrooms (whichever was greater), for each site. As with the threshold criteria set for surveys, we conducted analyses on all data available, and then conducted sensitivity checks by reducing the sample to those that met these criteria.

---

25 Pianta, La Paro, & Hamre (2008).
26 We also considered using Teaching Strategies GOLD as an outcome. **See the "Exploring Teaching Strategies GOLD as an Outcome Measure"** section for more information on why we did not conduct analyses using it.
27 Mashburn et al. (2008).
28 Cunningham & Stanovich (1997).
29 The BUILD Initiative and Child Trends (2015); Connors & Morris (2015).
30 CLASS data were primarily collected from the 2015-16 school year. For classrooms missing CLASS scores in 2015-16, we accepted data from the prior or following year (i.e., 2014-15 or 2016-17). Approximately 80 percent of the final CLASS data used for analysis came from 2015-16.
31 Burchinal et al. (2010); Early et al. (2007); Office of Head Start, Administration for Children and Families (2013, 2014, 2015).
32 For this, we used model-produced site-level estimates (i.e., HLM empirical Bayes estimates), which became the outcomes in our final models, as described under the **"Relating Scores and Outcome Measures"** section. HLM models take into account shared variance among classrooms within the same site and use empirical Bayesian estimates to adjust estimates based on the number of data points and the reliability within each site.
33 Using raw data, the average site-level CLASS scores were very similar: 6.19 on Emotional Support (SD = 0.55), 6.07 on Classroom Organization (SD = 0.81), and 3.28 on Instructional Support (SD = 0.90).

FIGURE 1
Distribution of Site-level CLASS Scores

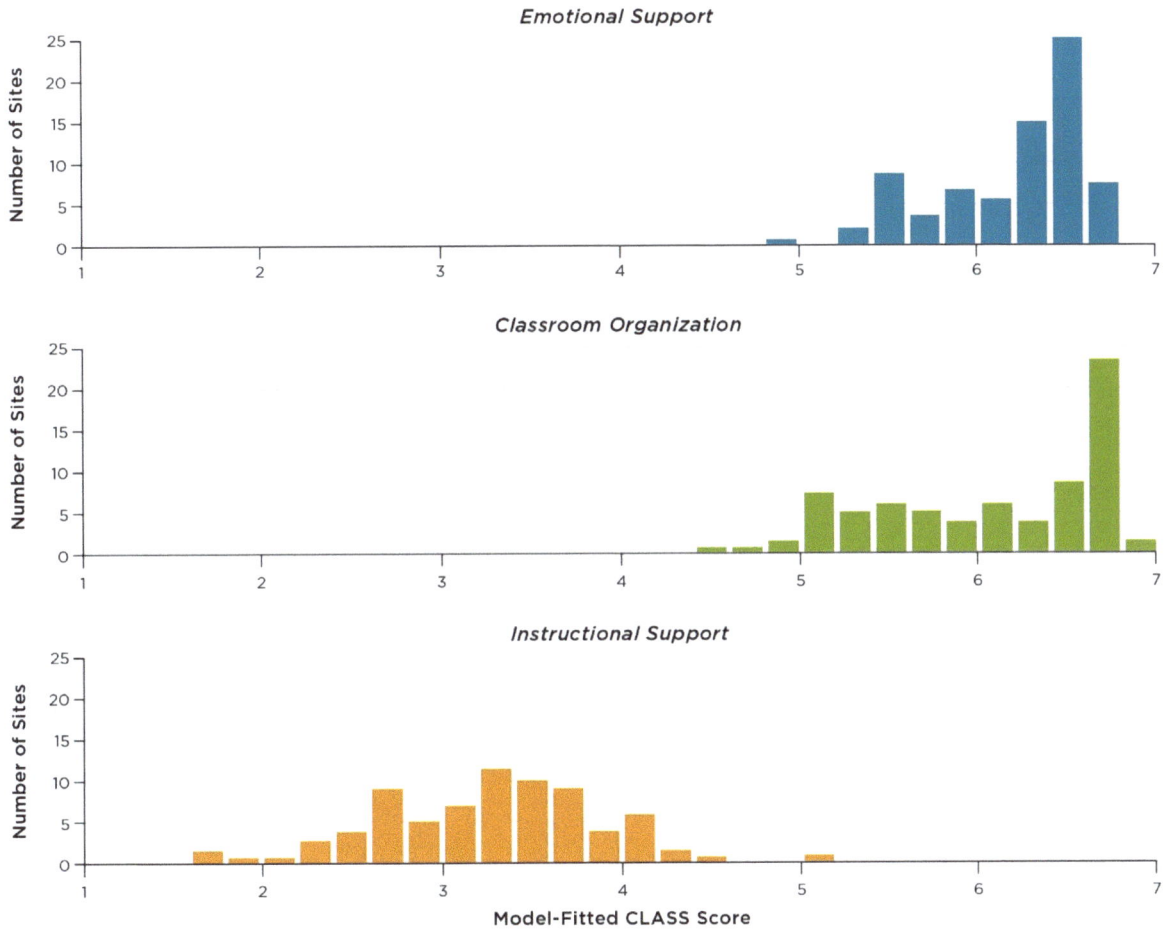

Note: Each site's CLASS score was obtained by fitting unconditional 2-level HLM with classroom scores nested within sites. The bin width is 0.2.

Student attendance. Data on the number of days attended and the number of total days enrolled in the 2015-16 school year were provided for all students enrolled in participating sites from CPS and DFSS attendance records. An attendance rate is calculated as the percent of days a student is present at school out of the total number of days that student is enrolled. A growing body of evidence suggests that student attendance is closely tied to a range of educational outcomes. Absenteeism is particularly high during pre-k, and is associated with poorer school attendance and learning outcomes in later grades, even after accounting for a variety of factors.[34] We therefore included attendance as a student outcome due to its importance for learning, and as an indicator of families' engagement with the preschool program.

A total of 9,094 students were included in available attendance data, of which about 60 percent were from 41 school-based sites and 40 percent were from 40 community-based sites. Modeled estimates of site-level attendance ranged from 67.4 percent to 94.1 percent, with an average of 85.2 percent (SD = 7.1 percent).[35] The intra-class correlation for student attendance was 0.374. **Figure 2** displays the site-level attendance rates.

---

34 Connolly & Olsen (2012); Cook, Crowley, Dodge, & Gearing (2015); Dubay & Holla (2015); Ehrlich, Gwynne, & Allensworth (forthcoming); Ehrlich, Gwynne, Pareja, & Allensworth (2014); Nauer, White, & Yerneni (2008).
35 See footnote 32 for how we derived modeled estimates. Using the raw data, the site-level average attendance was 82.5 percent (SD = 7.8 percent).

FIGURE 2
Distribution of Site-level Student Attendance Rates

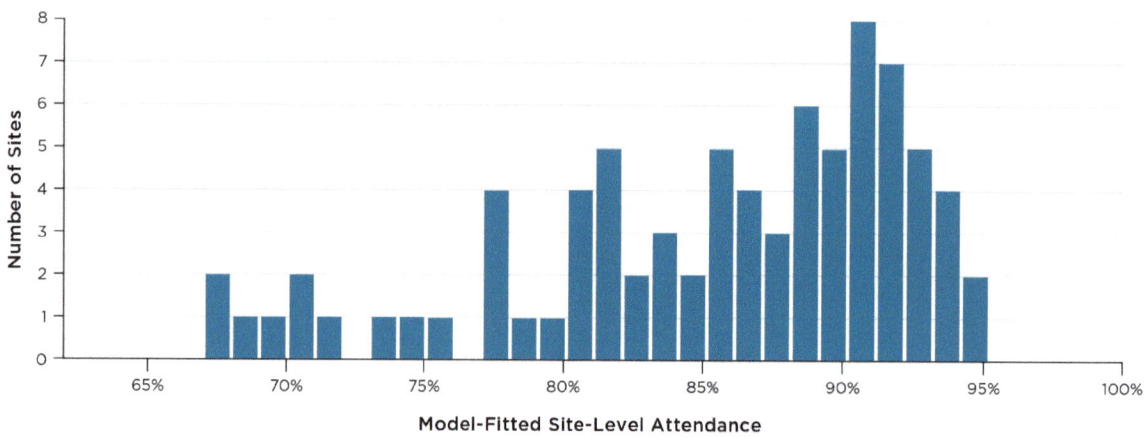

Note: Each site's attendance was obtained by fitting unconditional 2-level HLM with students nested within sites. The bin width is 1 percent.

TABLE 3
Stages of Analyses

Stage of Analysis	Description / Goal	Type of Analysis	Unit of Analysis
1. Survey Measure Development	Ensured survey measures included in subsequent analyses were reliable, unidimensional, sensitive, and interpreted similarly by different groups of respondents.	Rasch analysis Used each person's responses on the survey to look at how the survey measures themselves functioned, and created refined measures.	Person-item responses to surveys
2. Creating Site-Level Measure Scores	Took the scores from Stage 1 and aggregated them up to the site level for each measure. Examined whether there was enough similarity in responses on a measure within a site compared to how people respond across different sites (intraclass correlation).	Hierarchical linear model (HLM)	Person scores nested within sites, producing site-level estimates for each survey measure
3. Grouping Survey Measures Into Essential Scores	Used site-level measure scores from Stage 2 to determine how the measures fit together with each other to condense a large number of measures into general organizational areas (e.g., leadership, parent involvement).	Theory, alignment with K–12 organization, and factor analysis	Site-level measure scores
4. Relating Essential Scores and Outcome Measures	Explored the relationship between essential scores (from surveys) and outcomes, at the site level.	HLMs that examined whether site-level essential scores were related to differences across sites on their outcomes	Site-level essential scores, as predictors, entered at level 2 of HLM

Analyses

We first present a description of all analyses, followed by the results of each set of analyses.

Our validation study ultimately asked whether site-level survey responses on the *Early Ed Essentials* were related to two site-level outcome measures that have been shown to be meaningful indicators of early childhood education quality, as described above. However, this required several stages of analyses and preparation of the survey data themselves to obtain the most parsimonious and well-structured survey measures. **Table 3 on page 12** outlines the steps of analyses and the unit of analysis at each step.

Survey Measure Development with Rasch

A prior publication describes the development and initial analysis of the surveys.[36] The surveys are intended to measure specific features of ECE sites that literature has suggested are important, such as Teacher-Teacher Trust and a positive learning climate. By combining teachers' responses on multiple survey items together, we created survey measures, each of which represented a particular construct. Responses to items within each measure were analyzed using the Rasch IRT model (**see "What is Rasch"** section for more detail).[37] Rasch theory posits that questions of varying degrees of difficulty (in this case, ease or difficulty to *endorse*) differentiate people's placement along a developmental scale: Endorsing more difficult questions means the respondent is associated with higher levels (or more positive beliefs) on the underlying construct. **Figure 3** shows the structure of the surveys with a set of survey items that were all designed to measure aspects of "Program Coherence."[38] Rasch analyses help us empirically gauge whether survey respondents answer items in patterns that indicate items do in fact fit together to measure a single construct.

FIGURE 3

Structure of the *5Essentials* Surveys, Upon Which the *Early Ed Essentials* were Built

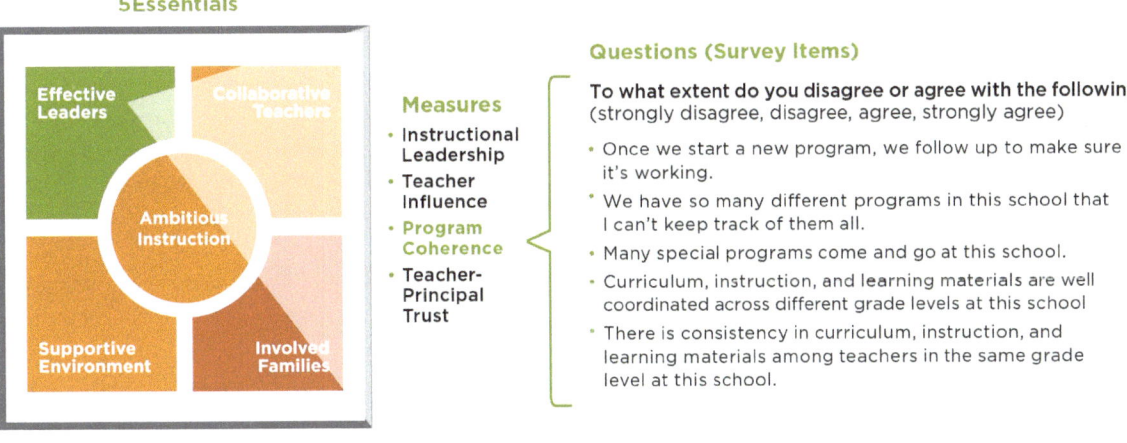

---

[36] Ehrlich et al. (2016).
[37] Wright & Masters (1982).
[38] Our use of questions and measures was modeled after the K-12 *5Essentials* surveys.

What is Rasch?

The items on the *Early Ed Essentials* surveys were created with the Rasch model in mind. Rasch analysis, from the Item Response Theory (IRT) framework, is used to help ensure that all of the items within a measure are measuring people's responses on a single scale, that people's responses are being measured reliably, and that the measure can precisely capture the perspectives of people all along the scale continuum. All analyses were conducted using the Rasch model, with Winsteps Rasch Measurement Program, Version 3.90.2.[A, B]

Why use Rasch analyses?

Several methods can be used to produce unidimensional survey measures (e.g., factor analysis, principal component analysis, IRT). However, we used the Rasch model, a type of IRT model. IRT models are preferred over raw-score analyses (e.g., simple means of response code numbers) for a variety of reasons:

1. *IRT creates measures that are on linear scales.* Survey item response categories are not linear. For example, the difference between "strongly disagree" and "disagree" on a 4-point Likert scale is *not* necessarily the same as the difference between "disagree" and "agree", so it would be a mistake to treat the category codes as numbers and do arithmetic with them, as raw score measurement models do. Instead, IRT creates linear measures from the counts of responses in categories, which is on a completely unbounded scale of –infinity to +infinity. These scores are provided on a scale called "logits" or a log-odds ratio.

2. *IRT provides a person standard error.* IRT provides an indication of the precision of each person measure (the inverse of the person standard error). Calculated on a large number of data, persons who hold attitudes that are near the average item difficulty will have low standard errors, meaning that we are more confident that the person's calculated measure is very close to the person's actual attitude. Large standard errors indicate large amounts of error variance, which contributes to low reliability. When analyzing survey results, the estimation can be made more efficient by adjusting for the varying amounts of measurement error.

3. *IRT handles missing data.* Survey responses often include missing data. IRT permits these missing data without introducing bias into the measures, although it does reduce precision (increase measurement error). Use of raw scores does not permit missing responses without introducing perturbations of the scores.

The Rasch model. The Rasch model is a simple, more restricted form of IRT (compared to a 2PL or 3PL model) that estimates only one item parameter—difficulty. Use of the Rasch model requires selection of questionnaire items that fit this more restricted model. In contrast, more complex IRT models use additional item parameters to fit the model to the data. While one disadvantage of Rasch analysis is that some items may need to be discarded or modified to fit the model, there are multiple advantages over other IRT models for the development of surveys to be used longitudinally in education settings:

1. *Rasch places person measures and item difficulties on the same scale.* Placement of both person measures and all item difficulties on the same scale permits us to make direct inferences about a person's performance relative to the scale of items. In the case of questionnaire data, this enables us to easily predict a person's responses to all items in a measure given the person's measure. For example, we might say that a person with a measure of 1.0 logits is expected to agree with the two hardest items and strongly agree with the other items. Although the logit measures are not meaningful themselves (and scales will vary from one measure to another), being able to state expected responses enables us to concretely describe any particular measure value.[C]

2. *Rasch allows for comparisons over time.* The measures can be easily equated across different samples of respondents, permitting us to track changes over time. If the slope parameter has to be considered as well, as is the case with other IRT models, the equating procedure is much more difficult, requires much more data, and is less stable.

WHAT IS RASCH?...*CONTINUED*

Using Rasch helps ensure reliability, and construct and internal survey validity.
Rasch output provides abundant information about the function of our measures. Of primary importance during our validation study was that our measures were *reliable*: That what we were measuring captured the *true* response (or experience) of the respondent. In other words, responses to survey items did not have large amounts of random error. Rasch reliability coefficients also help us determine whether the questions in the measure have enough precision to differentiate across people who hold different opinions about a construct.

Internal validity can be confirmed by testing the unidimensionality—or that all questions are measuring a single construct—of the set of questions and by confirming the fit of the data to the model. The Rasch model calculates an expected response for each person to each item, and the degree to which people and items in the aggregate are acting in accordance with expectation produces measures of fit. Fit statistics included in the output help determine whether there are questions measuring a concept *other than* the one being assessed by the other questions in that measure (indicating that we should perhaps reject the presumption of unidimensionality). We may increase the internal validity of measures by removing questions not related to the concept being measured, or by adding questions that enhance the definition of the concept. We use the item fit statistics, along with correlations between questions, to verify that our measures only include questions that are measuring the degree to which people endorse a single, underlying concept. Analogously, a person with a poor fit statistic ("large misfit") is likely someone who is responding in unexpected ways. We are likely to be skeptical of the measure from a person with a large misfit statistic; to adjust for this in analyses, we can inflate the standard error of the person to reflect our uncertainty about that person's measure score (see description of the measurement model used in our analyses).

A Linacre (2015).
B See https://bit.ly/RaschOverview for an overview of the Rasch model and its benefits for survey development.
C For survey responses, item difficulty can be understood to mean the difficulty of endorsing a particular item.

After data collection was complete, we made adjustments to our teacher and parent measures, according to their statistical and theoretical properties, to create refined measures for analysis.[39] In particular, we used Rasch to attend to the following characteristics to inform the creation of the final analytic-versions of the measures:

1. **Person reliability,** which indicates that the survey items are written in a way such that responses can be trusted to provide consistent information across respondents. High levels of Rasch person reliability indicate that the survey items are capturing the "true" response (or experience) of respondents, and do not contain high amounts of noise. Measures generally should have reliability of at least 0.70,[40] but reliabilities greater than 0.80 are preferred.

2. **Item fit** within the measure (infit mean square < 1.30), which indicates whether items fit together as measuring a single underlying construct. In our revisions, items with large misfit were removed from measures, unless they were the hardest item within the measure and increased reliability by measuring people at the top of the distribution well.

---

39 The initial measurement analyses and revisions on the teacher survey were conducted using data collected from both our validation sites as well as all other teacher responses throughout CPS (additional teacher survey responses n=2,748). In the first stages of our analyses, we were only concerned with individual person responses, without regard for the sites in which they taught. Rasch analyses were conducted on this larger sample for measure revision purposes. Having more teacher survey respondents provided us with more precise information about how items within measures worked.
40 Nunnally (1978).

3. **Spread of difficulty** the items are able to capture, which indicates whether items within a measure are able to capture the full range of beliefs by respondents. We assessed this by visually inspecting output that mapped item difficulty against person difficulty to see which measures had limited spread. We also examined difficulty to ensure we did not have items that had similar difficulty levels and therefore differentiated people similarly. In those cases, we removed redundant items for parsimony.

4. **Differential item functioning (DIF),** which compares responses between individuals in different groups. For our purposes, we examined DIFs between settings (school- versus community-based settings) and people completing the parent survey in different languages (English vs. Spanish). This helped us understand whether all the items were understood by different groups of survey-takers in similar ways. Items with significant ($p < 0.05$) and large ($p > 0.50$) DIF contrasts were considered for removal.[41] In several cases, items with large and significant DIFs were left in the measure if those items did not misfit *within* each group. For example, large DIFs across types of settings indicated that the item appropriately fit with all other items for teachers within each setting, but across settings teachers may have had a very different experience about the question being asked—precisely something we wanted to tap into using these surveys. We also examined whether the order of difficulty across the items was consistent within each setting type, another indication that while levels of responses might have been different across settings, the items themselves fit appropriately within the measure.

In making our final decisions about which items to keep in each measure, we also considered theory and practice (e.g., keeping an item that we felt was critical to measuring the construct at hand and would be particularly useful information for programs when they received their survey results) as well as our goal of alignment with the existing *5Essentials* surveys being used in schools and districts across the country (e.g., we might keep a redundant item if it kept the measure consistent with what K-12 teachers receive on their surveys). These efforts and decisions led to the refined survey measures used in the next stage of analyses—with 24 measures and 122 items from the teacher survey and 9 measures and 42 items from the parent survey. The names of these measures are included in **Tables A.1 and A.2 in the Appendix**.

Creating Site-level Measure Scores

Once we finalized our measures and scored all respondents in our validation sample,[42] we used hierarchical linear modeling (HLM[43]) to create measure scores for each site in our study (i.e., site-level measure scores). These analyses were conducted for each measure on the teacher and parent surveys.

Since each measure has its own standard error, using it without adjustments results in heteroscedasticity in the level-1 error term: $Measure\_score_{ijk} = \pi_{1jk} + e_{ijk}$, where $e_{ijk} \sim N(0, \sigma^2_{1jk})$. Dividing through by the standard error removes the heteroscedasticity: $Measure\_score^*_{ijk} = Measure\_score_{ijk}/StandardError_{ijk}$, resulting in the following 3-level model:

Level 1:
$Measure\_score^*_{ijk} = \pi_{1jk}\left(\frac{1}{StandardError_{ijk}}\right) + e^*_{ijk}$, where $e^*_{ijk} \sim N(0, 1)$

---

41 Linacre (2015) suggests looking at both significance and severity of differences, looking for DIFs where there is less than a 5 percent likelihood that DIFs are detected by chance and where DIF contrasts are at least 0.50 logits. We used the Rasch-Welch probabilities to examine significance.

42 Final scoring was based on data from the validation sample alone (see FN 39) to determine the scoring parameters (item and step difficulties) for the measures. Therefore, the scoring was based on a representative sample and not overly influenced by the disproportionately large number of school-based respondents by including the full CPS teacher sample.

43 Bryk & Raudenbush (1992).

Level 2:

$$\pi_{1jk} = \beta_{10k} + r_{1jk}$$

Level 3:

$$\beta_{10k} = \gamma_{100} + u_{10k}$$

π_{1jk} represents an individual person's adjusted measure score. The β_{10k} in the level 2 model represents the average measure score across all people at site k, and r_{1jk} is individual-specific residual. At level 3, individuals are nested within their sites, such that γ_{100} represents the overall average measure score across all sites plus a residual for each site (u_{10k}). Overall, this three-level measurement model adjusts for person error (at level 1), accounts for the number of respondents per site (i.e., sites with fewer respondents are considered less precisely measured and so their scores are constrained to be more similar to the overall mean than sites with more respondents), and allows for shared variance among people clustered in the same site. These provide model-predicted site-level measure scores (accessible through each school's deviation from the mean, or u_{10k}), which differ from straight averages because they account for shared variance across people and make the individual person measure scores more precise by adjusting for that person's error on that measure.

Examining Site-level Characteristics for Each Measure

Because the *Early Ed Essentials* surveys were designed to provide site-level information to school- and community-based ECE leaders, staff, families, and other stakeholders, it was important that each measure be able to differentiate *across* sites. One way to test this was to calculate the intraclass correlation (ICC) for each measure. Technically, it is a ratio of the variance between sites vs. within sites; for example, ICC = 0.10 means that 10 percent of all the variance is between sites while 90 percent is within sites. The ICC examines each person's responses on the survey to see if their responses are *more* related to that of others in the same site and *less* related to responses from people in different sites. The higher the ICC, the more there is a difference in responses across sites relative to differences among people within the same site. In other words, the teachers/parents within a site share something in common that differentiates them from teachers/parents in another site. For the purposes of our validation analyses, we were trying to see if survey responses could detect between-site differences; the bigger the ICC, the easier those differences will be to detect. Typically, an ICC of 0.05 or greater is considered high enough to assume some level of shared variance within sites. **Tables A.1 and A.2 (in the Appendix)** include ICCs for each of our measures.

With responses to the survey now aggregated to the site level, we could also examine site reliability. Site reliability gives us a sense of how certain we can be that a school's score represents the true level of a construct at that site. When site reliability is high for a survey, then each school's average score on that survey can be used to determine whether it is significantly different from any other school because you are better able to trust those scores. Reliability is affected by both the number of respondents and the homogeneity of each school.[44] Unlike individual reliability or measure reliability as measured by Cronbach's alpha, there is no generally agreed upon cutoff for evaluating site reliability, instead often relying on an adequate ICC.

Grouping Measures into Essential Scores

Information about individual survey measures may prove useful for in-depth reflections among ECE staff, leadership, and families. However, to help provide an overview of how sites are doing on their organizational supports, we followed practices of the existing K-12 *5Essentials* survey and grouped measures into broader

---

[44] Feldt & Qualls (1999).

categories called essential supports (or "essentials"). By grouping measures into a small number of essentials, which capture a category of supports programs need in place to be successful, we can provide a simple and straightforward picture of the strengths and key areas of improvement for each site.

The grouping of measures into essentials was conducted largely based on theory, with a careful eye toward alignment with the existing K-12 *5Essentials* surveys. However, we began this work not knowing whether the structural nature of survey responses would match our theoretical organization of the constructs. For instance, the way the constructs related to each other may have been different than we anticipated. In particular, while we theorized that constructs from the parent survey might fall under different essentials,[45] we were not sure if that would be appropriate given empirical evidence. This was similarly the case for new measures included on the teacher survey.

To address these concerns, our final placement of measures under essentials for the validation analyses were also informed by an empirical examination of the structure of survey responses by using factor analyses. Since our final goal was to understand whether site-level survey scores related to site-level outcomes, we conducted the analyses using site-level measure scores. Factor analysis is a set of statistical procedures used to examine the underlying structure of correlations among different variables.[46] Specifically, factor analysis identifies a relatively small number of common "factors," or underlying constructs, that explain how different variables (i.e., survey measures, in our case) are related to one another. The analysis generates factor loadings for each variable, indicating the extent to which that underlying construct is related to that variable. By examining which variables load heavily onto particular factors, the analyst can interpret what each factor represents, or what the underlying construct is. For instance, if variables such as "vocabulary" and "reading comprehension" are heavily loaded onto one common factor, we may interpret this factor being about "verbal ability."

We employed exploratory factor analysis (EFA) to examine how our measures loaded onto common factors. EFA uses all the data available to identify the most suitable number of latent factors that can explain the covariance of measures and produces output on how each measure loads onto each factor. We chose EFA, rather than confirmatory factor analysis (CFA) or principal components analysis (PCA), since our aim was to let empirical evidence suggest a set of common factors underlying our measures.[47] As there is a good theoretical ground to believe that these underlying factors (i.e., essentials) interact with one another, we used oblique rotation in our EFA, allowing factors to be correlated with one another. We specifically used a form of extraction known as principal axis factoring. This method was chosen because it outperforms maximum likelihood extraction of factors in accuracy when there are equal loadings of variables on factors, random variation in loadings of variables on factors, or relatively weak factors.[48]

We ran three rounds of EFA on the teacher and parent survey measures across the 81 sites, varying the number of factors being extracted (from four to six) to see how this changed "grouping" of the measures. We compared the loadings from the most appropriate EFA to our theoretically-hypothesized classification of measures into essentials, leading us to make final adjustments as presented in the **"Results"** section.[49]

---

45 See Ehrlich et al. (2016).
46 Fabrigar & Wegener (2011).
47 Confirmatory factor analysis is suitable when "the researcher has a theory that clearly specifies a precise number of factors and exactly which measured variables each factor should influence" (Fabrigar & Wegener, 2011). Principal component analysis (PCA), though similar with factor analysis in many aspects, is primarily for data reduction rather than identification of latent constructs, and hence does not serve our purpose.
48 de Winter & Dodou (2012).
49 We used the factor analyses in this way, rather than calculate a factor score for each essential based on how each measure loaded on each factor.

Calculating Essential Scores

The decided-upon groupings of measures were then used to create essential support scores for each site. Recall that each measure is scored in logits and is on a different scale from one another; therefore, we first standardized each modeled site-level measure score to put them all on the same scale. We then averaged the set of measures under each essential support to create site-level essential scores. For example, each site had an Effective Instructional Leaders score that was an average of Instructional Leadership, Program Coherence, Teacher Influence, and Teacher-Leader Trust (**see Figure 4**). Each measure score, therefore, contributed equally to the essential it was categorized under (rather than using weights based on factor analyses). Calculating scores this way is more intuitive for practitioners to understand. It also highlights the importance of all the constructs that fall under an essential, each of which contributes something unique to that essential.

The essential scores were standardized across all sites, one more time, for ease of interpretation of our final analytic model results. These then became the predictor of interest in our final validation models, described in the following section.

Relating Scores and Outcome Measures

We examined the relationship of the essential scores to two outcomes: 1) teacher-child interactions, as measured by the CLASS Pre-K and 2) student attendance, using HLM. HLM allows us to appropriately model the relationship between a site's essential scores (e.g., Effective Instructional Leaders) and its student outcomes (e.g., attendance rates). As was the case with survey responses, HLM models entities nested within larger groups (e.g., students in schools) by taking into account the shared variance within each group. All analyses were conducted using all data available. Sensitivity checks were conducted on the sample of programs that met our threshold criteria (**see Tables A.4 and A.5 in the Appendix for results**).

For each outcome (CLASS Pre-K and attendance), we ran two HLMs looking at the relationship between survey essential scores and site-level outcomes. First, in order to understand the direct relationship between each essential and outcome, we ran unadjusted models nesting CLASS scores/attendance within site and included essential scores as the only site-level predictor at level 2. For our second model, we added student compositional characteristics for each site at level 2 to account for differences in the students being served by each ECE site. This told us the relationship between site's essential scores and outcomes above and beyond anything being driven by the population characteristics of children they serve.

CLASS Pre-K

We examined the relationship between a site's essential scores and its average CLASS score on each of its three domains (Emotional Support, Instructional Support, and Classroom Organization), with models conducted separately for each domain. CLASS scores were standardized across all classrooms before being entered into models. The unconditional model is as follows:

Level 1:

$CLASS\ Score_{ij} = \beta_{0j} + r_{ij}$

Level 2:

$\beta_{0j} = \gamma_{00} + \gamma_{01} Essential\ Score_j + u_{0j}$

where i represents a classroom in site j because CLASS scores are available at classroom level. β_{0j} represents the average CLASS domain score of site j; γ_{00} represents the expected CLASS domain score for a site with the average level of the essential being considered; and γ_{01} represents association between a site's essential score and its deviation from the average CLASS score—this is the coefficient of interest.

Sites differ in the students they serve, and this may confound true association between a site's essential score and its expected outcome. Thus, as described above, we controlled for these compositional differences in our modeling. Our goal was to take into account systematic differences among sites that past research has shown can be related to initial outcome status, so that we could more clearly see relationships between organizational conditions and outcomes that were not due to who was being served in each program. In other words, we wanted to control for differences in sites due to non-malleable factors (i.e., background characteristics of who was enrolled in each site) and only see how much of the remaining variability, which might have been affected by changes in policy and practice, our surveys could predict.

In determining the appropriate covariates to include in our model, we checked to ensure our model did not contain covariates that were collinear. To check collinearity, we examined correlations among potential sets of covariates and our measures; this helped to ensure that our results would not show a spurious relationship between essential scores and outcomes. Our final model adjusted for the following set of compositional characteristics: racial composition (integrated, predominantly Latino, predominantly Black, or racially mixed) and share of students whose primary language is not English. We tested the inclusion of a poverty indicator, but it was highly correlated with the composition variables.[50]

With the level-2 specification now including several covariates, γ_{01} represents the association between a site's essential score and its expected CLASS score, adjusting for demographic composition of the site. In other words, the model now considers the association within subgroups of sites that share similar demographic compositions. Similarly, γ_{00} now represents the expected CLASS scores for a site with an average level of each essential serving the "average" composition of students. u_{0j} now represents each site's remaining difference on their CLASS scores that is not explained by its essential score or observed demographic composition.

Attendance

The model applied to CLASS scores was also applied to study the relationship between a site's essential scores and its average student attendance, as measured on a scale from 0 to 100 percent. An important difference is that the level-1 unit is a student rather than a classroom. In this case, γ_{01} represents the association between a site's essential score and a site's deviation from the average student attendance: If the estimate of γ_{01} is, say, 2, then the model suggests that one-standard-deviation increase in the essential score is associated with 2 percentage point increase in the site's expected attendance rates. In addition to the covariates added in the CLASS models, we included age (percent three-year-olds) because prior research shows that attendance is higher among four-year-old students than three-year-olds.[51] Level-1 specification remained same as in the CLASS models, so β_{0j} and r_{ij} still represent each site's average and an individual student's deviation from that average, respectively.

---

50 Because our intention was to understand the relationship between essential scores and outcomes in all sites, we did not control for the type of setting of each site, nor for covariates that were strongly related to setting. Therefore, some potential covariates, such as percent students with disabilities, were excluded because they differed greatly between school- and community-based settings. Entering these into the model, therefore, would largely serve as a proxy for a site's setting and simply test the difference between settings.
51 Ehrlich et al. (2014, forthcoming).

Results

Survey Measure Characteristics

The final analytic versions of all measures on both the teacher and parent surveys were highly reliable, with most showing reliabilities above 0.80, suggesting the items provide a consistent measurement of individual parents' and teachers' beliefs about the construct being examined. In regards to evidence of internal validity, the infit mean squares were in an acceptable range (> 0.7, < 1.3) for all measures. **Tables A.1 and A.2 in the Appendix** provide Rasch-produced person reliability scores for each measure. However, there were very high rates of extreme (positive) responses on most of the parent survey measures, indicating that we did not have a sufficient number of items that were "difficult" for parents to endorse and thus to differentiate parents' beliefs and experiences.

Tables A.1 and A.2 in the Appendix also provide an overview of DIFs on the final versions of each measure. The tables share the number of items with significant and large DIFs. For the teacher survey, DIFs are reported for respondents in school vs. community-based sites. Eighteen of the 24 measures had one or no items with significant and large DIFs. The measure with the most DIFs (4 of 4 items) was a measure of school commitment; we advise to monitor how this measure functions in the future. For the parent survey, school vs. community-based DIFs were explored as well as DIFs by language of survey administration (English vs. Spanish). There were no items with significant and large DIFs by agency on the parent survey and only one measure with more than two items with language DIFs (a measure called Including Parents as Partners).

Site-level Measure Characteristics

Tables A.1 and A.2 in the Appendix also show the ICC for each measure on the teacher and parent surveys, respectively. On the teacher survey, the measures with the lowest ICCs are those that ask about instruction or child-child interactions, while almost every other measure has an ICC > 0.10. Each of these low-ICC measures focuses on something that occurs *within the classroom*; thus, it might not be surprising that they don't hold together as a site-level construct. For example, for an ICC to be higher on the measure Early Mathematics Development, there would have to be more site-by-site differences (across schools or community-based sites); instead, the low ICC indicates that there are actually just as many differences between *teachers* or classrooms within a site. We continued to use these measures—as combined into their corresponding essentials—in our validation analyses, but note this as a potential problem for detecting relationships with outcomes. This makes sense, as each teacher is reporting on what is happening within his or her classroom, and not about a construct that is school- or center-wide. This may also suggest that individual practice within the classroom may be less pervious to the decisions being made at higher levels (e.g., the curriculum being implemented). On the other hand, when teachers are asked about Teacher-Teacher Trust, there appears to be something about working in a particular site, or in how the items are phrased, that influences teachers' responses to that measure—teachers in the same site have more similar responses to each other than teachers from different sites. If the ICC had been low for Teacher-Teacher Trust, it would have indicated that teachers have dramatically different impressions of how much they trust one another within a site. Our parent survey measures have low ICCs overall. This means that the survey did not differentiate across sites well based on how parents felt about these concepts. Discussion about ongoing efforts to revise the parent survey are presented in the *Discussion and Implications* chapter.

Factor Analysis Results and Categorization of the Measures into Essentials

We entered our factor analysis with an already-existing theoretical placement of measures into essentials, and then used the factor analysis results to refine these placements. We identified the most informative version of EFA (tested with 4-6 factors) based on grouping patterns (e.g., whether a factor has sufficient number of meaningful loadings) and statistical considerations such as Kaiser rule (each factor should explain more variability than an individual variable can) and factor correlations (factors should not be too highly correlated).[52] Based on these criteria, we determined the most appropriate number of factors was five.

Table A.3 in the Appendix presents the factor loadings that resulted from the EFA. Overall, the results indicated that: 1) almost all measures from the parent survey correlated strongly with one distinct factor; 2) teacher measures hypothesized to fall under Effective Instructional Leadership clustered together and showed close connection with measures in Collaborative Teachers, in that they loaded strongly onto the same factor; and 3) measures hypothesized to fall under either Ambitious Instruction or Supportive Environment correlated highly with another factor.

We took into account our EFA findings and considered how they aligned with the way measures are categorized under essentials for the K-12 *5Essentials* surveys. In cases where many measures loaded onto a single factor but were separated into two essentials on the K-12 version, we erred on the side of keeping the structure similar to the K-12 version for future alignment. However, because the parent survey measures appear to bring a very different perspective, we added an essential for exploration called "Parent Voice." **Figure 4** indicates the measures that were situated within each essential for the purpose of validation study analyses and presents the definition of each essential.

---

[52] Instead of letting a single criterion drive our decision, we took into account various factors to be more faithful to our exploratory aim (Osborne & Banjanovic, 2016).

FIGURE 4
Measures Included in Final Versions of the *Early Ed Essentials*

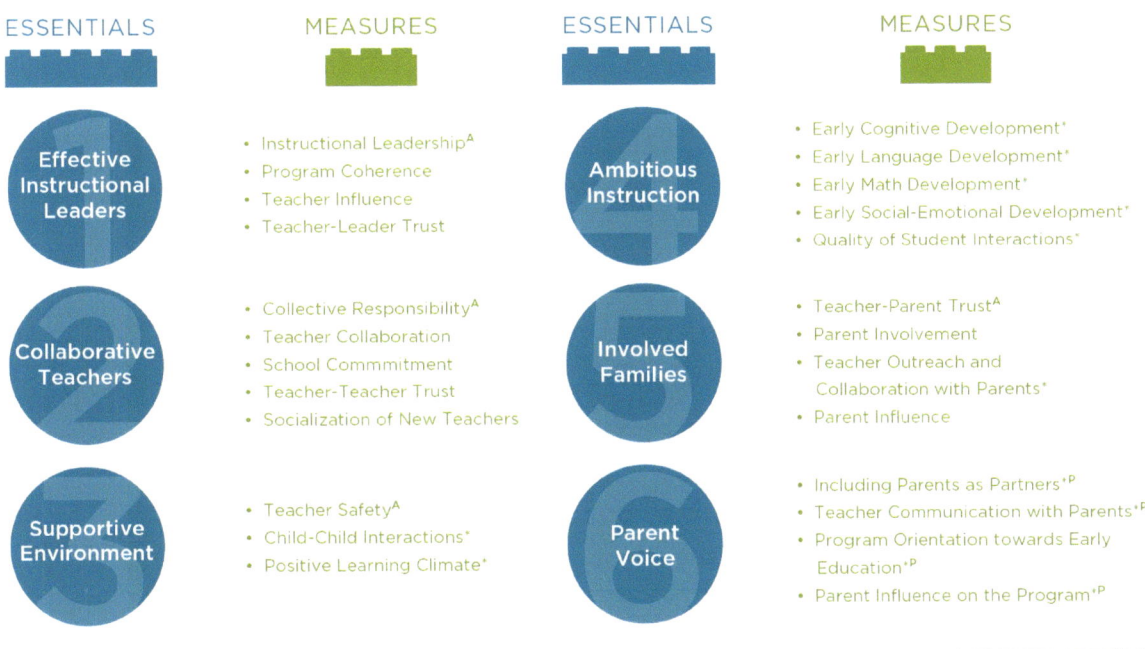

Note: * New Early Ed measure (not on K-12).   A Slightly adapted from K-12 measure.   P Parent survey measure.

1. **Effective Instructional Leaders:** The school or program leadership is strategically focused on children's development and early achievement. They nurture trust, collective understanding and responsibility for excellence, and improvement among staff and families.
2. **Collaborative Teachers:** Teachers are committed to the school or program, build strong relationships with their colleagues, and work together continuously to improve teaching and learning.
3. **Supportive Environment:** Schools or programs are physically and emotionally safe and engaging environments, wherein staff hold high expectations for children's social-emotional and academic learning, coupled with nurturing, individualized support for children and families.
4. **Ambitious Instruction:** Teachers and staff provide consistently engaging, effective, rigorous, and developmentally-appropriate curriculum and instruction.
5. **Involved Families**: Staff develop strong, collaborative relationships with families and support active family engagement in children's learning.
6. **Parent Voice:** Parents feel included as a partner in their child's learning and development, including influence over the programming.

Site-level Essential Scores

Essential scores were created by taking the average of all the standardized measure scores comprising that essential. For example, each site had an Effective Instructional Leaders score that was an average of Instructional Leadership, Program Coherence, Teacher Influence, and Teacher-Leader Trust.

We explored how different essentials related with one another by examining their correlations (**Table 4**). Results showed particularly high correlations between Effective Instructional Leaders and Collaborative Teachers. They both also related fairly well to Involved Families, suggesting these essential supports work together to create the overall culture and climate within an ECE site. Interestingly, Parent Voice showed relatively low correlations with other essentials. Combined with factor analysis results discussed above (that parent measures form a distinctive factor), this seems to indicate that parent perspectives may differ from those of teachers and staff.

TABLE 4
Correlations among Essential Scores

	Effective Instructional Leaders	Collaborative Teachers	Ambitious Instruction	Supportive Environment	Involved Families	Parent Voice
Effective Instructional Leaders	1.00	0.84	0.32	0.46	0.71	0.29
Collaborative Teachers		1.00	0.36	0.47	0.68	0.25
Ambitious Instruction			1.00	0.58	0.56	0.20
Supportive Environment				1.00	0.62	0.21
Involved Families					1.00	0.26
Parent Voice						1.00

We also looked at the percentage of sites that had high scores (i.e., in the top quartile) on each of the essentials. **Figure 5** shows the distribution of sites based on the total number of essentials for which they had top-quartile scores. More than one-third of all sites did *not* have scores in the top quartile on *any* of the essentials. Another one-quarter had strong top quartile scores on only one essential. It is notable that 21 percent of sites were in the top quartile on three or more essentials. This percentage is very close to that found in the original study of the five essentials survey in which 20 percent of schools were in the top quartile on three or more essentials.[53] A careful examination of the combinations of strong essentials also revealed that programs with Effective Instructional Leaders scores in the top quartile *always* had Collaborative Teacher scores above the median (in the upper 50 percent). This is not surprising given the high correlation between Effective Instructional Leaders and Collaborative Teachers; however, it does remind us of the close and positive relationship between these two overarching constructs.

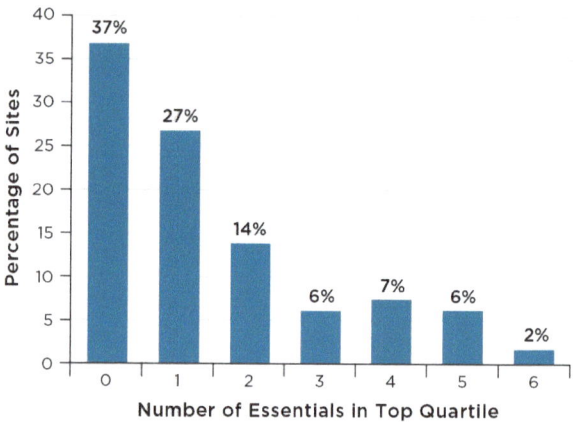

FIGURE 5
Distribution of Sites with High Scores on Essentials

Relationships between ECE Site-level Essential Scores and Outcomes

Relationships between Essential Scores and Teacher-Child Interactions (CLASS scores)

We separately examined the relationship between essential scores and CLASS domain scores for each site: Emotional Support, Classroom Organization, and Instructional Support. **Figures 6a–c** show CLASS scores for sites that had scores in the bottom and top quartiles (representing the weakest and strongest scores) on each essential. Two essentials—Effective Instructional Leaders and Collaborative Teachers—were significantly related to all CLASS domain scores. For example, sites with the weakest Effective Instructional Leadership scores, based on survey responses, had an average CLASS Instructional Support score of 3.02. In contrast, sites with the strongest Effective Instructional Leadership scores based on survey responses had an average CLASS

---

[53] Bryk et al. (2010).

Instructional Support score of 3.56, which is equivalent you a 0.83 standard deviation difference. However, Ambitious Instruction had the opposite relationship with CLASS outcomes—in particular, it trended toward being significantly negatively related to Emotional Support.

FIGURE 6.A-C

Effective Instructional Leadership and Collaborative Teacher Essential Scores Were Significantly Related to Early Childhood Education Sites' CLASS Scores

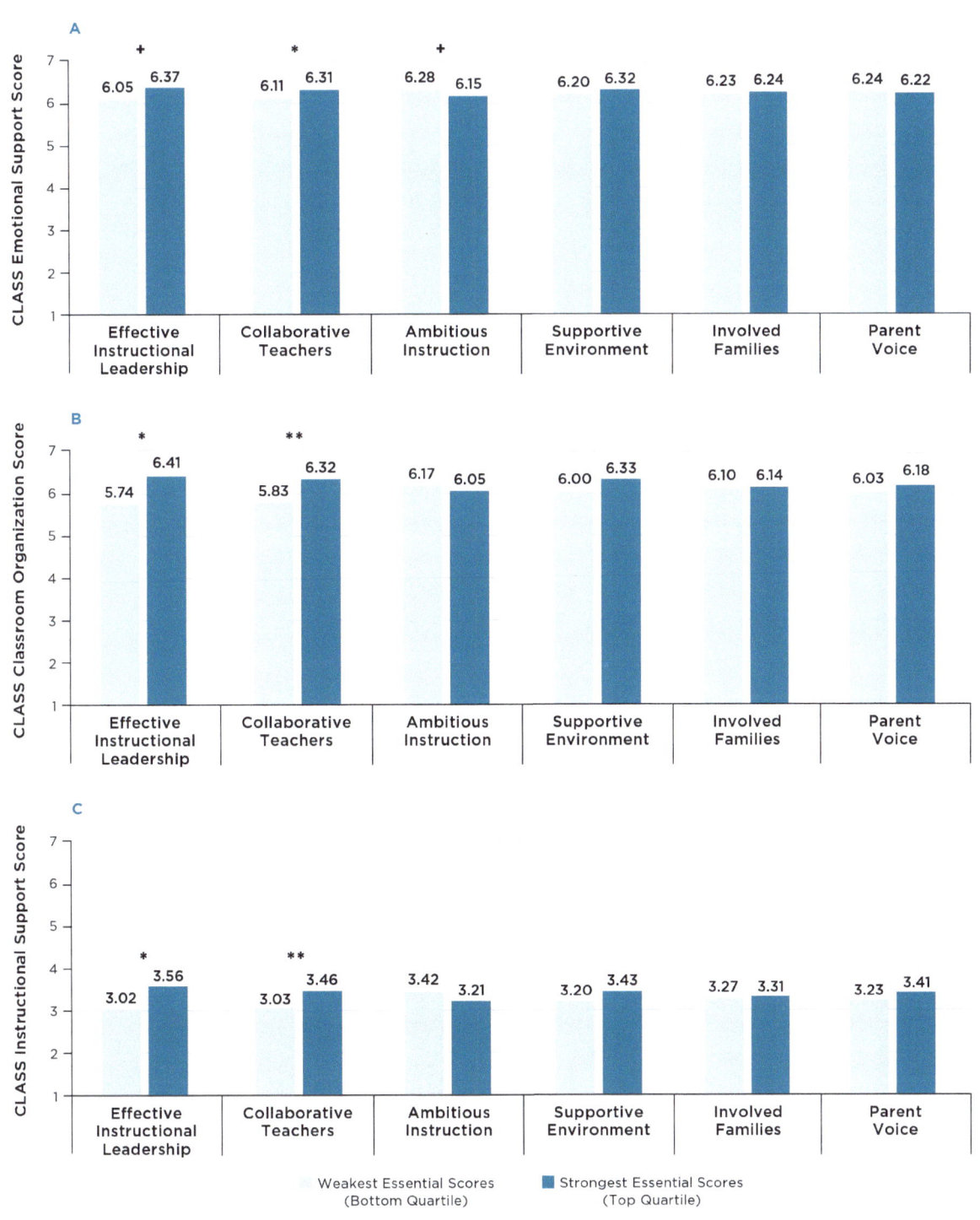

Note: Each pair of bars compares average CLASS scores with essential scores in the bottom vs. top quartiles. Each site's CLASS score was obtained by fitting unconditional 2-level HLM with classroom scores nested within sites; these model-fitted scores were then used to produce the top/bottom quartile average score. + indicates that the relationship between the essential score and the outcome is statistically significant at the $p < 0.10$ level; * indicates significance at the $p<0.05$ level; ** indicates significance at the $p<0.01$ level; *** indicates significance at the $p<0.001$ level.

As shown in **Table 5**, when we controlled for the characteristics of students enrolled in each site (i.e., adjusted model), most significant relationships remained (albeit were slightly diminished). This means that the positive relationships between Effective Instructional Leaders/Collaborative Teachers and CLASS Instructional Support and Classroom Organization domains held true regardless of the student population.

Relationships between Essential Scores and Student Attendance

Similar models explored relationships between site-level essential scores and student attendance rates. Four essentials were significantly related to student attendance—Effective Instructional Leaders, Collaborative Teachers, Involved Families, and Supportive Environment. Without controlling for the background characteristics of students enrolled in each site, a 1 standard deviation difference on each of these essentials corresponded to between 2.38 and 2.94 percentage point difference in average attendance rates between sites (**Table 6**). **Figure 7** shows what attendance rates were for sites with the strongest and weakest essential scores, based on the surveys. For example, sites with the strongest Supportive Environment scores had an average attendance rate of 89.5 percent, compared to 81.8 percent for sites with the weakest Supportive Environment scores. This 7.7 percentage point difference can add up to a lot of extra days of instructional time. For example, let's suppose there are 180 days in the school year. On average, students in sites with strong Supportive Environment scores attended pre-k for an additional 13.9 days over the year—two and a half weeks more instructional time spent in school for each student. Multiply this by the number of students in a site, and you can see how this quickly adds up to a meaningful difference in the number of additional days of learning within a site.

In the adjusted models, the significant coefficients were reduced somewhat, but still significant. For example, the relationship between Effective Instructional Leaders scores and attendance changed from 2.73 to 1.86. This means that the relationships between the essentials and attendance may have partially resulted because both stronger essentials and better attendance are more common in schools serving particular student populations. By controlling for student characteristics, the coefficients from the adjusted models were comparing the relationship of the essentials with attendance net of the influence of the student characteristics.[54]

TABLE 5
HLM Coefficients Relating Essential Scores to CLASS Scores

| | Emotional Support | | | | Classroom Organization | | | | Instructional Support | | | |
	Unadjusted		Adjusted		Unadjusted		Adjusted		Unadjusted		Adjusted	
	CoE	P-Val	CoE	P-Val	CoE	P-Val	CoE	P-Val	CoE	P-Val	CoE	P-Val
Effective Instructional Leaders	0.159	0.074	0.129	0.137	0.223	0.015	0.177	0.040	0.190	0.025	0.160	0.046
Collaborative Teachers	0.180	0.043	0.142	0.105	0.271	0.003	0.208	0.016	0.231	0.006	0.201	0.012
Ambitious Instruction	-0.149	0.086	-0.161	0.059	-0.099	0.279	-0.136	0.111	-0.130	0.117	-0.128	0.104
Supportive Environment	0.042	0.637	-0.024	0.812	0.116	0.210	0.025	0.802	0.060	0.483	0.008	0.932
Involved Families	0.020	0.826	-0.023	0.792	0.047	0.616	-0.020	0.823	0.045	0.599	-0.008	0.921
Parent Voice	-0.037	0.696	-0.035	0.700	0.041	0.680	0.035	0.698	0.069	0.448	0.079	0.353

CoE = Coefficient; P-Val = P-Value

Note: Each essential coefficient comes from a separate model in which only that essential was included as a predictor. Coefficients are presented in standardized terms. Unadjusted models do not include covariates; adjusted models control for racial composition (integrated, predominantly Latino, predominantly Black, or racially mixed) and share of students whose primary language is not English. The CLASS was standardized at the classroom level (within each domain) and then entered into the models. Model-estimated site-level SDs on the CLASS domains are (in standard terms): 0.70 (Emotional Support), 0.75 (Classroom Organization), and 0.66 (Instructional Support).

---

[54] This would be consistent with other findings on differences in attendance rates by race in Chicago (see Ehrlich et al., 2014).

TABLE 6
HLM Coefficients Relating Essential Scores to Student Attendance Rates

	Unadjusted		Adjusted	
	Coefficient	P-Value	Coefficient	P-Value
Effective Instructional Leaders	2.737	0.001	1.864	0.006
Collaborative Teachers	2.934	0.000	1.895	0.006
Ambitious Instruction	1.147	0.162	0.586	0.400
Supportive Environment	2.711	0.001	1.531	0.055
Involved Families	2.383	0.003	1.513	0.030
Parent Voice	1.155	0.155	1.077	0.105

Note: 1) Each essential coefficient comes from a separate model in which only that essential was included as a predictor. 2) Unadjusted models do not include co-variates; adjusted model controls for racial composition (integrated, predominantly Latino, predominantly Black, or racially mixed), share of students whose primary language is not English, and share of three-year-old students. 3) Student attendance was entered into the models in percentage values (e.g., 90 percent entered as 90). Model-estimated site-level SDs on student attendance was 7.15.

FIGURE 7

Student Attendance Rates for Sites in the Top and Bottom Quartiles on Each Essential

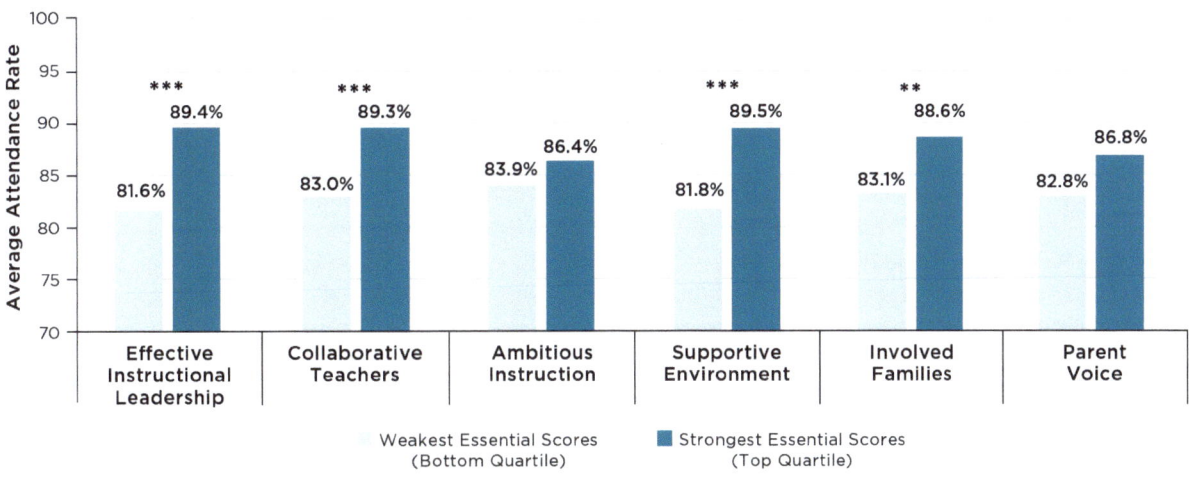

Note: Each pair of bars compares average attendance rates between sites with essential scores in the bottom vs. top quartiles. Each site's average attendance rate was obtained by fitting unconditional 2-level HLM with students nested within sites; these model-fitted scores were then used to produce the top/bottom quartile average score. * indicates that the relationship between the essential score and the outcome is statistically significant at the p<0.05 level; ** indicates significance at the p<0.01 level; *** indicates significance at the p<0.001 level.

Exploring Teaching Strategies GOLD as an Outcome Measure

During the course of this project, we obtained student-level scores from three time points over the year using the **Teaching Strategies GOLD Assessment System for Children** (TS GOLD). We explored the TS GOLD as a potential outcome for our validation analyses, but determined the data on our sample did not suit these needs.

The TS GOLD is a comprehensive, naturalistic observation-based assessment measuring knowledge, skills, and social-emotional behaviors.[D] In Chicago, the TS GOLD is the only universal kindergarten readiness assessment conducted for all students in publicly-funded pre-k programs. Teachers use the TS GOLD to track children's progress on 38 objectives at least three times per year. Objectives combine to create six internally-reliable scales: 1) social-emotional, 2) physical, 3) language, 4) cognitive, 5) literacy, and 6) mathematics.[E] Children who meet or exceed developmental expectations for their age on these dimensions are more likely to succeed academically in school, with lower levels of behavior problems in future years.[F]

The TS GOLD assessment system's intended use is as a formative assessment tool, meaning that it should be used to measure each individual child's progress toward a standard. The resulting information about each child's strengths and weaknesses is provided to teachers to be used to plan child-specific instruction. The system has been validated for individual children of the age range we were focused on (three to five years old) as well as with children who are English language learners.[G] While these past studies have found that the tool exhibits acceptable psychometric characteristics for individual children, the measure has not been used as frequently to investigate classroom or school effects, and its value as a measure of student skill, relative to direct measures, has been called into question.[H] Nevertheless we believed that the opportunity to relate school environment to growth in multiple domains merited the potential imprecision of the measure.

We first analyzed the longitudinal data of children enrolled at our sample sites between fall 2015 and spring 2016.[I] Importantly, we were only able to identify the site each child was enrolled in, but not the particular classroom or teacher each child was taught by. We observed generally high correlations in children's domain scores across the seasons ($r > 0.70$, $p < 0.001$). We also ran growth curve analyses to evaluate how much of the change in students' score over the year was attributable to within- vs. between-school components. We observed that the differences in growth scores that was explained by students being enrolled in different sites was relatively small (2.3 percent) compared to the amount that was explained by differences in students *within* the same sites (28 percent). This suggests that very little variation in scores is attributable to differences between sites (ICC = 0.076). This is in contrast to a previous study which was able to identify classroom differences in TS GOLD scores (ICC's between 0.185 and 0.591[J]).

We theorize, given prior research, that while there might be substantial classroom-by-classroom differences on TS GOLD growth scores for students, this might not translate as well at the site level. If classrooms within sites have different growth patterns, this would detract from getting consistent site-level growth scores. However, for the present study, where we were examining relationships between site-level survey responses to site-level outcomes, the low ICCs between sites indicated it would be difficult to find any relationships. Indeed, we nonetheless ran analyses of school level TS GOLD domain growth scores on each of the essential scores, but did not observe any significant relationships.

D   Lambert, Kim, Taylor, & McGee (2010).
E   Lambert et al. (2010).
F   e.g., Blair & Razza (2007); Clements & Sarama (2004); McClelland, Morrison, & Holmes (2000); National Early Literacy Panel (2008).
G   Kim, Lambert, & Burts (2013, 2014).
H   Miller-Bains, Russo, Williford, DeCoster, & Cottone (2017).
I   Analyses were conducted by Dr. Yoon Soo Park. For more information, see Park (2017).
J   Miller-Bains et al. (2017).

Differences Across Settings

It is crucial that as these surveys are developed and tested, we ensure they function properly in different early education settings—schools vs. community-based centers. In our earlier publication, we described our process for developing the surveys and the intentionality of conducting cognitive testing with a range of populations to make sure interpretations were similar among different groups of survey-takers.[55] In addition, under the *"Survey measure development with Rasch"* section, we highlighted how DIF analyses were used to confirm that the surveys were appropriate for use in both school-based and community-based programs. Indeed, the psychometric properties of our surveys indicate they are. In other words, people in different settings interpreted the survey items in similar ways.

However, it is possible that the experiences and perspectives of people across settings may differ. In other words, responses to the survey could indicate different levels of organizational support. Our study found just that: For Effective Instructional Leaders and Collaborative Teachers, survey scores were lower in community-based settings than in school-based settings ($p < 0.01$ on t-test). This was also true for our outcomes—CLASS scores and student attendance. Because the direction of differences was similar for essential scores and outcomes, this adds to confirmation that the *Early Ed Essentials* surveys were able to sort the sites in a reliable and valid way. In some cases, the relationship seen between essentials and outcomes may have been driven largely *by* these setting differences. However, future research on this is well warranted, particularly as larger sets of data are collected in various settings, to further explore the relationships between survey responses and outcomes *within* settings.

Summary

There is evidence that the measures included in the surveys were highly reliable, and most were able to differentiate among sites. When looking at the relationships between essential scores and outcomes, results showed that Effective Instructional Leaders and Collaborative Teachers were significantly related to interactions occurring within the classroom between teachers and students (i.e., CLASS scores). These same two essentials as well as two additional ones—Involved Families and Supportive Environment—were significantly related to student attendance. There were no significant relationships between Parent Voice and site-level outcomes, and slightly negative relationships between Ambitious Instruction and site-level outcomes. The following chapter shares key findings from a qualitative study conducted on a set of ECE schools and community-based centers with high and low survey scores. This deep qualitative work, as will be described, provides evidence that the surveys picked up on meaningful differences between sites.

---

[55] Ehrlich et al. (2016).

CHAPTER 2
Qualitative Validation Study

The previous chapter highlights that responses to the *Early Ed Essentials* surveys follow a pattern that is related to other measures of ECE engagement and quality: School- and community-based ECE sites with stronger organizational conditions also have better CLASS scores and student attendance. This chapter presents key findings from a qualitative study conducted to explore additional evidence on the *discriminant validity* of the surveys—in other words, whether the surveys are distinguishing between ECE sites with qualitatively different on-the-ground climate, structures, and practices. These findings make an important contribution to the field because they illuminate what these essentials look like in pre-k settings and provide concrete descriptions of the climate and conditions most differentiating ECE sites with strong and weak essential support scores. A forthcoming report will provide detailed evidence and discussion of findings from the qualitative study.

Qualitative Study Methodology

Research Questions

We asked whether there are qualitatively different, on-the-ground climate and conditions between ECE sites with high and low *Early Ed Essentials* survey scores. And, whether there are structures and practices that most differentiate sites with high versus low survey scores. Our aim was to provide "practical" validation for what the surveys measure by "directly comparing and contrasting quantitative statistical results with qualitative findings for corroboration and validation purposes."[K] If the survey data differentiates schools/community-based centers with strong and weak survey scores in the same ways the qualitative evidence does, then we have corroborating evidence of discriminate validity and greater confidence the surveys capture important aspects of organizational conditions and are sorting sites in a reliable and valid way.

Qualitative Sample

We purposely sampled four sites—two schools and two community-based centers—with *Early Ed Essentials* survey responses indicating strong and weak organizational supports.[L] Purposeful sampling is aimed at obtaining insight about a phenomenon with cases selected because they are information-rich and illuminative. We conducted preliminary Rasch analyses on *Early Ed Essentials* teacher and parent survey responses from 36 of the 81 validation study sites that had completed the surveys by April 2016. Using measure scores from both the teacher and parent surveys, we rank ordered the sites by each measure and identified schools and centers that ranked in the top and bottom quartiles of each measure. We then summed a count of the number of times each school or center fell within the top or bottom quartile across measures. Schools and centers with the greatest number of occurrences of being in the top or bottom quartiles were rank ordered and used to create the recruitment lists. Qualitative data collectors were given two lists from which to recruit four sites. List A contained the top eight ECE sites (four schools and four community-based centers) that were most frequently ranked in the top quartile across all measures. List B contained the bottom eight ECE sites (four schools and four community-based centers) that were most frequently ranked in the bottom quartile across all measures. Data collectors were blind to which list, and thus which sites, had been categorized as "strong" or "weak" based on their survey responses. A recruitment email was sent to the school principal/community-based center director inviting participation in the qualitative study. Of the eight schools and community-based centers on List A (later revealed

QUALITATIVE STUDY METHODOLOGY...*CONTINUED*

to be sites from the bottom quartile), five did not respond to the recruitment email, one initially agreed to participate but did not respond to subsequent planning emails, and two agreed to participate. Of the eight schools and community-based centers on List B (later revealed to be sites from the top quartile), four did not respond to the recruitment email, one declined participation, one initially agreed to participate but did not respond to subsequent planning emails, and two agreed to participate.

Methods, Participants, and Procedures

We conducted site-visits lasting three consecutive days between May and June 2016, specifically May 16-18, May 23-25, June 6-8, and June 13-15. During each site visit, we employed three data collection methods: 1) individual interviews of leaders and teachers and group interviews of family members; 2) observations of common area environments, activities, and interactions; and 3) photographic documentation of common area spaces and displays. We designed a unique protocol for each method to capture in-depth information about what the essential supports look like and feel like in the school/community-based centers' early childhood program.

Administrator, Lead Teacher, and Assistant Teacher Individual Interviews

We conducted 33 individual interviews of staff, including six leaders (1-2 per site), 26 teachers and teacher assistants (6-8 per site), and one guidance counselor. Individual interviews were conducted in person and lasted approximately one hour each. Site administrators recruited a minimum of six (maximum of 10) ECE classroom lead and assistant teachers to participate in individual interviews during the school/community-based center day. Prior to participation, each staff member completed informed consent procedures. The individual interview protocol elicited information from staff about the ECE program vision and goals, program coherence and communication, shared leadership, teacher and leader capacity building, instructional guidance and feedback, children's learning, relationships and trust, family engagement, and resources for improvement, as well as emergent themes generated by participants themselves. All individual interviews were digitally audio-recorded and transcribed verbatim for analyses.

Parent Group Interviews

We conducted group interviews of 33 family members (6-10 per site) who had preschool-age children enrolled in the school/centers' early childhood program. Group interviews were conducted in person and lasted approximately one hour each. Site administrators and family engagement staff recruited a convenience sample of a maximum 10 family members to participate in the group interview. Flyers in English and in Spanish, containing a short explanation of the study, were made available to administrators. Prior to participation, parent group participants completed confidentiality agreements to ensure they would not share with others what they or other members said during the group interview. The group interview protocol elicited information from family members about the ECE program's site leadership, climate and environment, outreach and communication to families, family involvement activities, relationships and trust, children's learning and kindergarten transition, as well as emergent themes generated by participants themselves. At one site, the parent group interview included a mix of Spanish-only speaking and bilingual Spanish-English speaking members. For this group, a native bilingual Spanish-English speaking data collector was available to co-facilitate and translate questions and responses during the group interview. All group interviews were digitally audio-recorded and transcribed verbatim for analyses. The bilingual Spanish-English group interview was translated verbatim by a bilingual transcriptionist.

Observation and Photo Documentation

We observed common areas for an average of seven hours per site (range 6-12 hours) across the three-day visit. Common areas were defined as ECE student drop-off and pick-up areas, administrative offices, hallways, gymnasium, and outdoor activity areas. An observation protocol structured documentation of interactions occurring among adults and between children and adults, as well as the photographs to be taken of displays and information posted in the common areas.

QUALITATIVE STUDY METHODOLOGY...*CONTINUED*

Analyses

Interview, observation, and photographic data were analyzed through three iterative cycles of coding: 1) descriptive, 2) thematic pattern, and 3) conceptual model building.

Data Preparation and Inter-rater Reliability Procedures

Individual and group interview transcriptions were checked for accuracy and uploaded to NVivo software for qualitative analyses. Researchers read each interview and focus group transcript multiple times and coded responses into appropriate question banks using NVivo. In order to ensure inter-rater reliability when coding interviews, observations, and photos, researchers individually applied descriptive and thematic codes and then co-reviewed selected interview transcripts, observation protocols, and photos. Where coding discrepancies occurred, researchers discussed rationales for coding decisions until consensus was reached as to how to code the text segment or data element. This information was then used to enhance inter-rater reliability in future coding efforts.

Descriptive, Thematic Pattern, and Conceptual Model Coding Procedures

Descriptive coding was utilized to summarize passages of qualitative data in short phrases. Examples of descriptive codes include: *Factors that Influence Quality, Instructional Strategies Implemented, Shared Leadership and Teacher/Staff Influence, Data Use on Teacher Practice and Classroom Environment, Parent Involvement,* and *Parent Influence.* A codebook for descriptive coding was developed that provided the code name, to what interview questions the code was mapped, a description of the code, and inclusion/exclusion criteria. This type of coding led to a categorized inventory of the individual and group interview data's content and set the groundwork to extract themes that emerged from the data. Pattern coding was used to organize thematic patterns that describe phenomena in the qualitative data related to specific research questions. Data was extracted from NVivo and organized in additional ways, including Excel, Word tables, and word-clouds to further examine patterns across the data. Examples of thematic codes include: *Teacher-Parent Respect and Relationships, Opportunities for Teacher Collaboration, Improvement in Teacher Practice, Ambitious Instruction,* and *Parents as First Teachers.* Following thematic pattern coding, conceptual models were developed by linking themes and emergent codes generated from the first two cycles of analysis to create higher-level understanding about the actions, perceptions, and processes that reflect the degree to which the essentials were present at each site and what factors facilitated and hindered the presence of the essentials.

K Creswell & Plano Clark (2011).
L Palinkas, Horwitz, Green, Wisdom, Duan, & Hoagwood (2015).

Findings

As mentioned, a forthcoming report will provide detailed discussion of evidence and findings from the qualitative study. Here we provide top-line findings and illustrate key themes for each essential support using a handful of quotes from leaders, teachers, and families. Please note, that at the time of the qualitative study design and data collection, we did not have the quantitative evidence indicating that a subset of parent survey measures functioned best as its own essential, now titled Parent Voice. Therefore, the qualitative study was designed to capture information on the five essentials from the original framework: that is, Effective Instructional Leaders, Collaborative Teachers, Supportive Environment, Ambitious Instruction, and Involved Families. This qualitative analysis does not present findings separately for the Parent Voice essential; rather, it integrates the parent perspective as evidence to better understand each of the essentials in action and, in particular, the Involved Families essential.

The experiences observed and heard about though site visits supported the quantitative validation findings that the teacher survey strongly differentiates across programs that provide stronger vs. weaker organizational supports for staff, children, and families. Researchers who were blind to which sites had high and low essentials scores found evidence that easily discerned differences in site climate, structures, and practices emblematic of strong and weak organizational supports. Those differing conditions matter greatly to the actions of leaders, teachers, and families experiencing them regularly. Simply put, sites with strong organizational essential supports create contexts far more supportive of teaching, learning, and family engagement than sites with weak organizational essential supports. Strong essential supports enabled and encouraged the work staff engage in daily with each other and with children and families. Conversely, weak essential supports disabled and discouraged that work. And, for families, sites with strong essential supports paved the way for partnership and influence in their child's early education, whereas sites with weak essential supports relegated families to the periphery.

In sites with high survey scores, staff held common understandings of their goals as an early education program that were guided by their leader's strong purpose-driven vision that was rooted in child developmental science and developmentally-differentiated practice. Leaders in these sites established only a few strategic priorities, built emotionally-encouraging relationships with staff, and set up structures that protected time for cross-classroom collaboration. These sites had a positive ambiance: interactions and conversations among staff and between staff and families were frequent, warm, and focused on offering one another encouragement around endeavors both professional and personal. Leaders used these relationships and routine discussions of practice to build a unity of purpose that activated a sense of collective responsibility, innovation, and efficacy among all staff for achieving the program vision. Leaders and staff emphasized the importance of children's social-emotional learning as the foundation for learning. All staff worked together diligently to create the most supportive environment they could for young children and families. They then used that growing sense of security, trust, and calm to expose children to new ideas and tasks, an engaging pedagogy that afforded children active learning opportunities. Undergirding all of this was the belief that partnerships with families was critical to effective teaching and children's success, including allowing parents input into higher-level instructional decisions. Families were able to articulate these beliefs and experiences as clearly as staff were. For example, parents in sites with high survey scores were knowledgeable and able to speak in detail about the nature of their child's classroom experiences and how impressed they were by teachers' persistence in helping their child develop and learn to their fullest potential. They also had a perspective on the relationships and collaboration among the staff. For example, parents shared stories about how confident they were that when they shared a concern with one staff member, a solution would be discussed among relevant staff members and put into practice consistently.

In contrast, staff in sites with low survey scores articulated their primary aim as making sure they complied with the myriad of program regulations consuming the focus of their leaders, including that children achieve program-established kindergarten-readiness goals. Leaders in these sites prioritized smooth operations. There was an absence of leadership practices and organizational structures that advanced a pedagogical-vision, coherently guided instruction, or allowed staff time to focus together on the work of teaching and learning. Teachers described how leaders interacted with them in highly transactional ways, including prescribing classroom schedules and teaching approaches, and assigning tasks to individuals. Staff kept to individual classrooms, interacting minimally with colleagues or families in the common areas and then only through brief, perfunctory exchanges. Teachers described poor curriculum alignment across the school/center, coupled with heavy emphasis on rote learning as the key strategy to building basic literacy and numeracy skills in preparation for kindergarten. These instructional weaknesses combined with weak commitments to the school/center, to innovation, to the benefits of partnering with families, and to persisting in meeting the needs of all children, especially those with special needs and English language learners. Staff pointed to children's lack of self-regulation as a barrier to their teaching and to children's progress, and for a subset of leaders and teachers, the belief existed that families caused the difficulties children experienced adjusting to the classroom. Undergirding all of this, in turn, were insubstantial involvement and relationships with families.

In the sections that follow, we present findings that describe and differentiate what the essentials look like in ECE schools and community-based centers with high and low survey scores. Evidence suggested that high survey scores corresponded to strong organizational essential supports while low survey scores corresponded to weak organizational essential supports. For each essential support studied at the time of the qualitative data collection—Effective Instructional Leaders, Collaborative Teachers, Supportive Environment, Ambitious Instruction, and Involved Families—we summarize major themes and illustrate leader, teacher, and family experiences and actions. These summaries and illustrations are then followed by tables highlighting the structures and practices within strong and weak sites that created the conditions and experiences described in those major themes and illustrations (**Tables 7-11**). For example, under the essential Collaborative Teachers we illustrate that teachers in strongly organized sites felt they were in a place where everyone was working together towards the same goals. The table that follows (**Table 8**) highlights the structures and practices leaders had established, including protecting time for and clarifying the purpose of collaboration. Those structures and practices created the conditions that allowed teachers to experience a sense of collective responsibility. More detailed evidence will be provided in the forthcoming report on the qualitative study findings.

Structures and Practices that Describe and Differentiate ECE Sites with Strong and Weak Organizational Essential Supports: Major Themes and Illustrations of Leader, Teacher, and Family Actions

Essential Support: Effective Instructional Leaders

Leaders of strongly-organized sites have a vision for the early childhood program that is purpose-driven and deeply grounded in child developmental science and developmentally-appropriate practices. This vision connects staff to the reasons they became early childhood educators and enables staff to trust leaders, and allows leaders to cultivate a unity of purpose among staff and with families. Leaders establish a few strategic goals, champion and focus direction continually, and influence and motivate action. Leaders cultivate a collaborative culture and strong professional learning community across all teachers, staff, and families that strengthens collective responsibility and action for change.

Reflecting on the importance of the leader's vision on her teaching, one teacher at a strongly-organized school shared:

> *I feel like it's empowering [here]... when it's not just from the top down. When its right here and we believe in this stuff and I have something to share and it's valued by your administrator. Then your co-teachers and your colleagues also buy in too and you have that energy and you have that love and then you have an administrator that pushes you in that way and supports you and guides you and nudges you a bit further. I think it's kind of what we try to do with our students too, now even when they're only three. So I think [the principal] leads by example for sure.*

Leaders of weakly-organized sites have a vision for the early childhood program that is focused on ensuring compliance to the myriad of program standards and funder requirements. As a result, leaders employ a transactional leadership style and micromanage staff. Monitoring teacher practice for compliance consumes leader interactions with staff. Families are included in the work only to the extent required by funders;

they are not partners in the learning community. Teachers often work in isolation, feeling as if they are watched all the time, yet still underserved by leadership.

When asked to reflect on what she needed from leadership, a teacher at a weakly-organized site reflected on how the leaders' compliance-focused vision felt like no vision at all:

I think leadership needs a vision or a focus... [Here] I have to ask, what's your vision for pre-K? Really, what is the vision? So that when we come to work every day we know that we are operating under this vision. And, if we come to you for support we'll let you know why what we're doing is in alignment with that vision. So I think someone constantly thinking about what pre-K needs. ... Then ask us, 'how are you guys going to meet this vision?' And tell us how [you] plan on supporting [us] to meet this vision. I know, it's just like a dream. I know. I get frustrated all the time because I'm like that's not going to happen here.

TABLE 7

Structures and Practices that Differentiate ECE Sites with High vs. Low Scores on Effective Instructional Leaders

EFFECTIVE INSTRUCTIONAL LEADERS	
Strong Essential Scores	**Weak Essential Scores**
1. Leaders communicate a vision that is purpose-driven and rooted in developmental science and developmentally-appropriate practice.	1. Leaders communicate a vision that is compliance-driven to the myriad of program standards and funder requirements.
2. Leaders pass along a small number of actionable goals, which are related to program standards but linked also to the vision. They problem-solve implementation issues with staff.	2. Leaders pass along written program guidance they receive with the expectation that staff will figure out how to change their practice to implement new requirements properly.
3. Leaders create a warm and professional work environment, expecting staff to focus on practice and cultivating children's love of learning.	3. Leaders create a rigid work environment, expecting staff to focus on procedural compliance to program standards.
4. Leaders maintain regular communication with staff, sending weekly updates to help staff prioritize time and to promote open dialogue about successes and challenges.	4. Leaders communicate only sporadically with staff, as needed to ensure staff compliance with standards and requirements.
5. Leaders' purpose-driven vision and actions helps staff connect to a moral purpose and the reasons they became early educators.	5. Leaders' compliance-driven vision and actions often overloads staff, as it makes it difficult for staff to prioritize time to focus on practice.
6. Leaders use a facilitative and relational leadership style to build trust, shared understanding, and collective responsibility.	6. Leaders use micromanagement and a transactional leadership style to hold individuals accountable for meeting standards.
7. Leaders create a culture and supportive policies to welcome family partnerships, supporting staff to ensure that families are involved, included, and influential in the program.	7. Leaders interact minimally with families and do not expect staff to outreach to families beyond formal family involvement activities that meet minimum program standards.
8. Leaders observe classroom practice routinely and provide performance feedback that is strengths-based. Staff all receive regular feedback.	8. Leaders observe classroom practice sporadically, and provide feedback that is compliance-focused and often deficit-based. Non-teaching staff may not receive any structured feedback.
9. Leaders cultivate a culture of collaboration, model reflective practice, and discuss teaching and learning regularly with staff.	9. Leaders cultivate a culture of individual accountability, and remind staff verbally and in writing of what constitutes procedurally compliant practice.

Essential Support: Collaborative Teachers

Teachers in strongly-organized sites collaborate with each other, leaders, and families to raise performance overall and increase children's learning. Leaders express confidence that with ongoing support and collaboration, teachers and staff will grow their knowledge and skills and be able to innovate practice that meets the needs of all children. As a result, teachers engage routinely in discussions of practice with both peers and leaders, and have time protected weekly and monthly for professional collaboration that builds their capacity. Collaboration opportunities are structured, informed by data, and focused on immediate problems of practice in order to improve children's learning. Leaders frequently join these collaboration times helping to shape and guide teaching and learning as staff review and use data, design instruction, and deepen content knowledge. Teachers have a sense of collective responsibility and feel encouraged in the face of daily challenges. They describe how critical conversations and planning with their peers are to their teaching effectiveness.

A teacher in a strongly-organized site reflected on how integral and unique professional collaboration was in her school's culture and practice:

> *In other schools I've noticed it's just the teachers sit in a room and learn but here it's the whole staff. [For example], when we were learning social emotional things about the students... everybody was here from the aides... [And] even our custodian sat in on a couple things. I think that's pretty remarkable and I know that it's unusual. That doesn't happen everywhere. But it's nice to know that...the things that we know are the best practices are being shared with everybody in the entire school.*

Teachers in weakly-organized sites do not engage in routine collaboration; they rarely have structured time for discussions of practice or peer learning. Improving practice is viewed by leaders as teachers' individual responsibility, which results in no systematic approach to improving teacher practice and children's learning. Teachers receive minimal active instructional guidance from leaders; rather, they are forwarded program guidance or practice requirements that leaders receive from funding agencies and departments. Although teachers may ask each other informally how to address a problem of practice, they do not have scheduled time to observe and receive feedback from, or collaborate with peers. As a result, teachers feel individually accountable but isolated and overwhelmed in their work.

In a weakly-organized site, a teacher shared how this missing piece frustrated her:

> *That's one thing that gets to me because there is no collaboration. I am used to going to another classroom and saying, 'Hey, I couldn't do it this way. Can you tell me how can I do it that way, or didn't that way work for you?' [But here] everybody is not even on the same plan. Everyone is not even using teaching strategies. That's what gets me too because if I have a problem with it and I want to compare, I can't.*

TABLE 8

Structures and Practices that Differentiate ECE Sites with High vs. Low Scores on Collaborative Teachers

COLLABORATIVE TEACHERS	
Strong Essential Scores	**Weak Essential Scores**
1. Leaders view collaboration as the key to build capacity and achieve their vision. They cultivate cultures of collaboration.	1. Leaders do not view collaboration as a solution for improving practice.
2. Leaders view supporting teachers' professional development as a responsibility shared by teachers and leaders.	2. Leaders view practice improvement as teachers' responsibility and speak openly about their frustration with teachers' performance.
3. Leaders ensure teachers have protected time to meet together routinely (i.e., weekly and bi-weekly).	3. Leaders rarely protect time for teacher collaboration, only facilitating this time to the extent mandated by program requirements.
4. Leaders ensure collaborative time has a clear purpose and is structured by goals, data, and protocols that allow teachers to demonstrate expertise and to learn from each other.	4. Leaders engage independently with funder-provided coaches and specialists, then pass along information to teachers in written memos as procedures teachers should follow.
5. Teachers use collaborative time to address variations in children's learning and outcomes by focusing on pedagogical issues, using data to examine practice, and designing innovations.	5. Teachers rarely use children's data to critically examine instruction. When they do, it is usually done independently and focused only on their own practice.
6. Teachers observe each other's instruction several times a year to learn about creative approaches.	6. Teachers are directed to go to leaders for assistance with addressing a problem of practice, rather than to peers.
7. Teachers bring up problems of practice, and are committed to raising performance overall, in their own work and in that of their peers.	7. Leaders cultivate a culture of individual accountability, and remind staff verbally and in writing of what constitutes procedurally compliant practice.

Essential Support: Supportive Environment

Leaders and teachers in strongly-organized sites work diligently to create emotionally supportive environments for children and their families in order to promote children's adjustment and early learning. Teachers and leaders reference child developmental science when describing how essential a positive learning climate and relationships are to children's ability to learn. Teachers describe how wide the range is of age-appropriate behavior, and how hard they work to individualize their interactions to children's temperament. Moreover, they believe their ability to create supportive environments in the classroom is boosted by positive relationships and communication between parents and staff; in other words, they act on the belief that environments in the early years must be supportive of both the child and the family.

A parent at a strongly-organized site described what this looks and feels like from the families' perspective:

> *Supportive environment? Definitely. It's not only from the teachers and the staff to the kids, or from the director down. It's not just for the kids. I think it funnels all the way up from the children to the parents... They want parents to be able to facilitate things on their own. They started a teacher assistant program and there are a couple parents who are participating in that... So you see it's a very encouraging environment to continue development for everyone and it never stops.*

Leaders and teachers in weakly-organized sites do not consistently cultivate child-centered, supportive environments, nor do they recognize the value of such environments to teaching and learning. Leaders and teachers were dismayed at the wide-range of children's social-emotional needs and expressed the belief that children's low levels of self-regulation limit their ability to teach key concepts and early academic skills children need to be ready for kindergarten. Many teachers remarked that children should be able to adjust to the classroom routine much earlier in the year than they do. A few staff felt that parents contributed to the difficulties children have separating at drop-off and entering the classroom calmly, and wondered if it would be better if parents did not enter the classroom.

This lack of focus on cultivating an age-appropriate supportive learning environment is evident in the frustration shared by one teacher regarding meeting the needs of diverse learners:

> [It's difficult] when you don't have a child that wants to participate: [a child] that's just stubborn and doesn't want to write... and doesn't want to cooperate. Again, it comes with a language barrier, and you have [children] that just sit there and look at you like, 'what are you saying to me?' So it becomes difficult... We have a child that's just all over the place. He doesn't talk. He's building up his words...but it becomes a barrier because [even though] he knows it and he could come in and show you everything...for him to sit down and do it, it becomes a problem. He's not going to do that because he can't sit down [and]...he can't hold the pencil.

TABLE 9

Structures and Practices that Differentiate ECE Sites with High vs. Low Scores on Supportive Environment

SUPPORTIVE ENVIRONMENT	
Strong Essential Scores	**Weak Essential Scores**
1. Leaders and teachers ensure families are welcome and invited everywhere in the building.	1. Leaders and teachers do not welcome families into classrooms or encourage them to be a part of daily activities in the building.
2. Leaders and teachers make the physical space of the school/center embody the leader's vision.	2. Leaders and teachers do not use the physical space to connect the work to their program vision.
3. Common areas are outfitted with child-friendly materials and visual displays of children's work.	3. Common areas have few-to-no child-friendly materials or displays of children's work.
4. Leaders both model and create the expectation that positive, emotionally-supportive interactions will occur between teachers and children; families and teachers; and among staff.	4. Leaders do not model or create the expectation that emotionally-supportive interactions will occur among staff and with families.
5. Interactions and conversations among staff and between staff and leaders is frequent, warm, and focused on offering one another encouragement around endeavors both professional and personal.	5. Teachers keep to individual classrooms, interacting minimally in the common areas with colleagues, leaders, or families, and through brief, perfunctory exchanges.
6. Leaders reinforce in their discussions with staff and families that children's social/emotional learning is the foundation of the program and necessary for all other learning.	6. Leaders reinforce in their discussions with staff and families the importance of basic skills development.
7. Teachers provide students with emotional supports to engage in inquiry and develop a love of learning.	7. Leaders and teachers express frustration with children's impulsiveness and social-emotional "issues" stating that the lack of self-regulation makes it harder for them to prepare children for kindergarten.

Essential Support: Ambitious Instruction

Informed by child developmental science and comprehensive early learning standards, teachers in strongly-organized sites emphasize social-emotional learning as the foundation from which all additional early learning is made possible. Teachers focus on developing children's love of learning and feelings of competence within the preschool setting and classroom. Teachers and leaders describe a culture of ambitious practice, including the use of early learning standards and formative assessment combined with active, engaging, inquiry-based learning opportunities. Instructional planning occurs in teams and uses multiple sources of data to identify children's learning goals and to plan differentiated instructional experiences. Families are offered a range of activities that extend learning into the home through active parent-child experiences.

A parent at a strongly-organized site communicated her confidence and appreciation in the early instruction her child was receiving by the preschool teaching staff:

They're willing to try and pull your child in different directions just to see what works. Nothing is concrete. It's like, 'Let's try it! Let's see how he does. We'll take data. We'll get back to you.' Parent-teacher conference comes and then they will tell you all the data that they collected and why this works or why it doesn't work, so that's really helpful. I've never seen anything like that.

Feeling pressured by leaders to prepare children for kindergarten, teachers in weakly-organized sites focus instruction on developing discreet literacy and math skills through rote instruction, regardless of children's individual needs. Teachers focus on preparing children for kindergarten, and report using rote learning activities and "practicing" kindergarten behaviors of walking quietly, name writing, and raising a hand to speak. They give families homework folders containing activity sheets to complete with their child, which are also focused on discreet skill building. Some teachers express feeling overwhelmed with meeting the needs of diverse learners, especially children with special needs and those who are dual-language learners.

A teacher at a weakly-organized site described the tensions she experiences instructionally that arose from different understandings of the aims of both preschool and kindergarten readiness:

I think that [kindergarten readiness] means being ready for a structured environment, having more behaviors that are conducive to the kindergarten classroom. Because [kindergarten is] transitioning a lot away from play and it's more teacher-facilitated, direct instruction. [Kids are] more accountable for [their] own learning. [But] I think for the [kindergarten] staff, or at least for the administration, it's all about being able to read and to come in with academic knowledge already. To me, it's more important that [children] have the behaviors first and [that they] understand the value of what school is.

TABLE 10

Structures and Practices that Differentiate ECE Sites with High vs. Low Scores on Ambitious Instruction

AMBITIOUS INSTRUCTION	
Strong Essential Scores	**Weak Essential Scores**
1. Leaders communicate that social-emotional learning is the foundation of the program and the curriculum for all students of all abilities.	1. Leaders communicate that discreet skill development is the focus of the program and the curriculum for all students of all abilities.
2. Teachers use assessment data to design meaningful learning opportunities that address diverse learning needs.	2. Teachers rarely if at all use assessment data to design meaningful learning opportunities. They are more likely to rely on activities in prepacked curriculum.
3. Leaders maintain student-teacher ratios below the maximum standard to allow for more one-to-one and small group instruction.	3. Leaders maintain student-teacher ratios at the maximum standard.
4. Teachers partner with families to develop meaningful learning opportunities at home.	4. Teachers give families homework folders to complete with their child that are focused on rote learning.
5. Leaders prioritize their time to provide teachers with guidance on teaching and encouragement to critically examine and improve practice and children's learning.	5. Leaders prioritize their time with monitoring compliance with funder requirements, and respond to teacher requests for assistance by referencing program standards.
6. Leaders install interdisciplinary teams that collaboratively do instructional planning. These teams use multiple sources of data on children's learning to identify needs at the classroom and school/center levels.	6. Teachers emphasize rote learning (e.g., number and letter identification; writing name; holding pencil and scissors) and are frustrated when students are not making progress.
7. Leaders establish and staff maintain a regular process to review data on teaching, learning, and family engagement.	7. Leaders check that lesson plans are submitted on time and contain all required information.
	8. Leaders and staff examine data on teaching, learning, only sporadically, and rarely collaboratively.

Essential Support: Involved Families

In strongly-organized sites, leaders' vision for the preschool program extends to the active engagement and partnership with all families. Leaders create policies that pave the way for families to be included, involved, and influential in the decisions related to their child's early education. Leaders and teachers create a welcoming and inclusive culture for parents. Leaders are at the entrance to the ECE program greeting and interacting with parents at drop-off and pick-up times. Teachers and families know each other's names even in situations when the child is not enrolled in the teacher's classroom. Leaders and teachers use every point of contact and both formal and informal communication to intentionally foster trusting relationships with families and to seek their input and feedback. Families are present in the building and knowledgeable about the program's goals and their child's experiences in the classroom. Families express appreciation, trust, and confidence in the intentions and capabilities of their child's teachers, the principal/director, and in the early childhood program overall.

At one strongly-organized site, the site leader explained how critically important she feels parent involvement is to successful early childhood education, expressing a desire to reach and involve every single parent with a child enrolled:

"I think it's essential that you put things into place to engage parents…for parents to understand what you're putting in place for their child so that they can carry it home every night and then every summer and then throughout year. Parents then also use us as a resource constantly. I'm getting phone calls from parents that have been here five,

seven years ago….But then I think about those parents that don't understand what we're trying to do and communicate. Every classroom that has had a family like that…we take that home with us….it's almost like a personal failure for us. Like, we're letting a family go out of this school that doesn't quite understand how important what we're doing is and what they should be doing is."

In weakly-organized sites, leaders and teachers do not consistently involve parents, nor is substantial engagement of families part of the guiding vision. Leaders have not created policies that pave the way for families to be included, involved, or influential in the decisions related to their child's early education. Drop-off and pick-up times are not used for sharing information, and in some instances teachers and families did not exchange a greeting. Leaders do not interact with parents and children during drop-off and pick-up times, and families typically were not present in the building outside of those times. Families had general knowledge of the classroom schedule, but less knowledgeable about their child's individual experiences or learning goals. Parents expressed frustration with the infrequent and perfunctory communication from leaders and staff, and were quick to state that teachers were doing the best they could with a tough job.

A teacher at a weakly-organized site expressed a sentiment about parents' presence in the building that was shared by many of her colleagues:

Parents make it harder. They're too—I'm not saying don't be attached to your child, but if you want me to help you, don't stand around for 30 minutes [when] they're crying. I understand you want to sympathize, and that's your child, but if you give me five minutes I can help them. But I can't help them while you're here because they only want you.

TABLE 11

Structures and Practices that Differentiate ECE Sites with High vs. Low Scores on Involved Families

INVOLVED FAMILIES	
Strong Essential Scores	**Weak Essential Scores**
1. Leaders champion the importance of family involvement and link it to the vision for program success.	1. Leaders do not highlight family involvement as an important element in their vision for program success.
2. Teachers and staff actively involve families, recognizing that families are integral to the work staff do to support children's adjustment to the school/center and advancing children's learning.	2. Teachers and staff rarely involve families proactively. Teachers are told to let leaders handle "issues" that families bring up about their child or the program.
3. Leaders and staff establish a regular process to support teachers with recruiting families for activities.	3. Teachers receive little, if any, support from leaders and staff to aid their family engagement efforts.
4. Leaders provide families a variety of formats and times of the day to be involved.	4. Leaders recruit families to attend monthly meetings as required by funders, and express frustration at low participation rates.
5. Leaders and teachers use multiple strategies for communicating with families about their children's learning and development.	5. Teachers and leaders communicate with families almost exclusively through written memos and newsletters, which parents often find to be impersonal and minimally useful.
6. Families learn ECE terminology and child development through conversations with teachers and at school/center family nights.	6. Families do not learn ECE and child development terminology.
7. Families learn about the curriculum and the concepts being explored with their child in the classroom and are asked to provide input.	7. Families may learn about the curriculum or the concepts being explored with their child in the classroom but are not asked for their input.

CHAPTER 3

Discussion and Implications

Prior research indicates that ECE programs with supportive organizational climate are more likely to exhibit higher-quality classroom structure and interactions.[56] However, the ECE field is lacking a measurement tool that allows programs to gauge the strengths and weaknesses of their organizational conditions. The goal of the present validation study was to examine the psychometric properties of the *Early Ed Essentials*—a recently adapted teacher survey and newly developed parent survey designed to measure organizational conditions of programs serving preschool-age students and families. Most importantly, this study examined whether site-level survey responses were related to teacher-child interactions (i.e., CLASS Pre-K) and student outcomes (i.e., attendance) at those ECE sites. In addition, we explored whether sites with survey responses indicating strong and weak essential supports have discernably different climate, structures, and practices as observed and described by leaders, teachers, and families within those sites.

Key Findings

Early Ed Essentials **measures are internally reliable and the teacher survey measures differentiate well across ECE sites.**

Overall, Rasch analyses indicate that the teacher surveys are able to reliably measure the staff who respond to them and can function well in both school- and community-based settings. In addition, intraclass correlation results suggest that the survey measures are sensitive enough to be able to detect differences across ECE sites. Measures on the parent survey, while reliable, do less well at differentiating across sites.

DIF analyses demonstrate that the surveys are being interpreted in similar ways for people in different groups—such as respondents taking the parent survey in different languages. These results provide evidence that the *Early Ed Essentials* surveys have the flexibility to reliably function across different types of center-based ECE settings (schools and community-based) and, for the parent survey, when administered in either English or Spanish.

Most essential scores relate significantly to site-level outcomes; however, parent survey responses do not.

Our study finds that some, but not all, of the organizational conditions measured by the *Early Ed Essentials* were associated in expected directions with other program-level metrics that are indicative of center-based ECE quality. Specifically, the essential supports of Effective Instructional Leaders and Collaborative Teachers were positively associated with scores on all domains of the CLASS measure of teacher-student interactions and instructional quality, providing evidence of the concurrent validity of these essential supports. The present study extends research identifying positive relationships between the quality of administrative practices of early childhood education leaders and the quality of the classroom arrangement and instructional materials and strategies teachers provide to children.[57] This includes recent research demonstrating the benefits of a professional development intervention to improve Instructional Leadership supports and professional

---

56   e.g., Burchinal et al. (2010); Dennis & O'Connor (2013); Rohacek et al. (2010); Whalen et al. (2016).
57   Lower & Cassidy (2007); Bloom (2010).

collaboration on children's outcomes in the area of social-emotional development.[58] This body of research literature and the present study findings indicate that measures of effective instructional leadership and routines of teacher collaboration within ECE settings could offer valuable information to organizations and programs for improvement. The *Early Ed Essentials* can identify potential organizational strengths and areas for development to guide efforts to improve conditions and thus advance the quality of teacher-student interactions and instruction.

Additionally, HLM analyses reveal a positive relationship between four of the essential supports examined in this validation study (i.e., Effective Instructional Leaders, Collaborative Teachers, Supportive Environment, and Involved Families) and student attendance. The addition of Supportive Environment and Involved Families as being positively related to attendance is telling. It is those organizational conditions that are most proximal to family and student engagement, which is likely represented well by student attendance. Associations between these organizational conditions in ECE settings and student attendance are particularly encouraging due to the growing body of evidence indicating that student attendance in the early years is closely tied to a range of educational outcomes. Specifically, absenteeism is particularly high during pre-k and is associated with poorer school attendance and learning outcomes in later grades, even after accounting for a variety of factors.[59] Research also shows that students living in poverty and who are racial/ethnic minorities have the highest absence rates.[60] Survey data on these organizational conditions can therefore provide information to ECE leaders, practitioners, and families that has the potential to lead to high-leverage strategies for increasing student attendance, which is critical for subsequent outcomes.

One important finding is that concurrent validity between the parent survey and ECE site-level outcomes was not confirmed. We also had evidence that the parent surveys were not adequately capturing a range of parents' perspectives, because so many parents responded extremely positively to items on the survey. This is consistent with other work attempting to measure parents' perspectives on their child's educational experiences.[61] As described in "Ongoing Areas of Survey Refinement and Testing" on page 44, we plan to build upon learnings from the qualitative work to inform future iterations of the survey for testing.

Sites with high and low *Early Ed Essentials* survey responses had qualitatively different climate, structures, and practices.

We found starkly discernable differences in the on-the-ground climate, structures, and practices in ECE sites with high and low *Early Ed Essentials* survey scores. Those differing conditions matter greatly to the actions of leaders, teachers, and families experiencing them regularly. Simply put, sites with strong essentials created contexts far more supportive of teaching, learning, and family engagement than sites with weak essential supports. Strong organizational essential supports enabled and encouraged the work staff engage in daily with each other and with children and families. Conversely, weak essential supports disabled and discouraged that work. And, for families, staff in sites with strong essential supports paved the way for partnership and influence in their child's early education, whereas sites with weak essential supports relegated families to the periphery.

---

58 Whalen et al. (2016). See also Rohacek et al. (2010) for evidence that classrooms with higher CLASS scores also had leaders reporting high expectations for their staff and allocating resources to build staff professional capacity.
59 Connolly & Olsen (2012); Dubay & Holla (2015); Ehrlich et al. (2014); Nauer et al. (2008).
60 Balfanz & Byrnes (2012); Ehrlich et al. (2014); Nauer et al. (2008); Romero & Lee (2007).
61 e.g., Bassok, Markowitz, Player, & Zagardo (2017); Hu, Zhou, & Li (2017); Meyers & Jordan (2006).

> The qualitative voice of families contributed substantially to our ability to describe and differentiate the climate and conditions of ECE sites with strong and weak essential supports.

Interviews are less-structured than surveys. Each open-ended question allowed parents an opportunity to respond with multiple reflections and examples, and to build off the reflections of other parent participants in the group. Parents shared experiences and perspectives that illuminated our understanding not only of the Involved Families essential, but for all of the essentials. We plan on applying the qualitative data and analyses to inform our ongoing efforts to revise the parent survey towards improved functioning. This is discussed in more detail in the next section.

Ongoing Areas of Survey Refinement and Testing

One essential—Ambitious Instruction—was consistently found to either not be related to program-level indicators of quality or to be negatively related to those outcomes. On the K-12 *5Essentials* surveys, the organizational condition of Ambitious Instruction is measured by asking students (grades 6 and above) about their experiences in their classes. As we developed the current *Early Ed Essentials* version, we explored numerous ways of designing survey items that would capture developmentally-appropriate instruction with high levels of expectation. The items tested in this version of the survey asked about the frequency with which teachers provided opportunities for children to practice particular skills. However, it might be the case that when asking about frequency of particular teaching tactics through teacher self-report, the items and measures were picking up on more "drill" type behaviors. Particularly difficult was designing questions that would capture practices that were developmentally appropriate, including providing high levels of emotional support. We plan to continue trying to improve our measurement of instruction through teacher self-report survey methods (e.g., possibly by measuring the guidance teachers receive around their instruction rather than self-report of their own teaching practices), but also concede that measuring the rigor and appropriateness of instruction and the types of expectations teachers have for children's learning may best be measured using observations.

We are also continuing to work on refining the measures and questions asked of parents. Parents responded to many items in extremely positive ways. We hypothesize that parents' generally positive responses can stem from a number of factors, including a lack of awareness of specific classroom conditions and parent cognitive dissonance with negatively rating programs to which they entrust the care and education of their young child. Through observations and interviews we conducted in strongly- and weakly-organized ECE settings, new ideas emerged for how parents and practitioners talk about and perceive organizational conditions. This qualitative exploration of on-the-ground organizational conditions is informing the development and testing new parent survey measures and items. Our goal in our parent survey revisions is to achieve greater spread across respondents and to design parent measures that measure unidimensional constructs and that are able to differentiate across sites. We have tried to achieve this goal by 1) referencing a specific staff role at the ECE program when possible (rather than asking more general questions), 2) describing what specific practices look and sound like, and 3) using response categories that rate the frequency of behaviors rather than categories that get primarily at agreement or satisfaction. In addition, we are further considering how some questions might be experienced differently by different groups of parents. For instance, some of our items and constructs were developed with the assumption that *all* families need the same supports from their child's ECE program. While there are some supports that all families may benefit from—such as being treated as a partner in educating their child—not all families need, or are looking for, guidance on how to develop their *own* skills or meet their families' needs (e.g., meeting education goals, finding resources on housing). Therefore, our newly-developed parent survey items are intended to be more sensitive to the varying perspectives and needs families have.

Policy, Practice, and Research Implications

The development of the *Early Ed Essentials* surveys holds broader implications for early childhood education policy, practice, and research. We lay here our hopes for contributions.

The early childhood education field will broaden the definition of "quality" to include organizational conditions and the important role of leaders as instructional guides.

For the ECE field, the theory behind the *Early Ed Essentials* and the data produced by the use of the surveys have the potential to contribute to how early childhood systems leaders and policymakers think about what high quality programing is. Broadening the definition of quality inherently can influence how programs and staff are incentivized, resourced, and supported. Recent research indicates that the majority of ECE policies, such as program licensing requirements and indicators within state Quality Rating and Improvement Systems (QRIS), focus primarily on "structural" features of the classroom and program (e.g., ratios, class size, teacher qualifications, and physical environment) and on health and safety practices.[62] Increasingly, policies targeting "process" aspects of ECE program quality, such as teacher-student interactions and instructional supports, have emerged (e.g., Head Start's designation renewal system's integration of CLASS benchmarks). Less prevalent are policies that focus on levers to strengthen the organizational conditions for continuous improvement, especially the professional learning environment and practice supports for ECE teachers and leaders, which research has shown both play central roles in improving the quality of teaching within the classroom and student's outcomes.[63] However, at this early stage of measurement development and research on the relationships of organizational conditions and outcomes within ECE programs, the authors would like to caution against the use of the *Early Ed Essentials* survey responses as accountability metrics themselves—at least until there is ample opportunity for the field to understand its use as an improvement tool.

Early education programs are able to generate actionable data and improvement planning tools that focus leaders' attention on strengthening the organizational supports for teaching and learning.

This framework and the availability of survey data can improve leaders', teachers', and other stakeholders' understanding of influences on teaching quality and students' outcomes that are at the organizational level, rather than driven at the classroom level. Data from the surveys have the potential to provide leaders and practitioners with actionable information to focus their attention on the specific organizational and Instructional Leadership supports that enable teachers and practitioners to be more effective in their daily work with children and families. Such information will aid program leaders in recognizing key organizational strengths and areas of improvement to more intentionally target, plan for, and implement improvement efforts. Furthermore, data from the *Early Ed Essentials* surveys has the potential to provide insights into program quality and practices from a parent perspective. Finally, such improvement efforts can be catalyzed through a shared vision and language that the framework of the essential organizational supports provides.

The *Early Ed Essentials* provides language about quality that aligns with how practitioners in elementary schools think about quality.

The K-12 education space has considerably more research and practice efforts focused on organizational conditions and climate. For instance, several states have included school climate surveys as a key non-academic indicator for their Every Student Succeeds Act (ESSA) plans. In addition, the *Early Ed Essentials* were

---

[62] Connors & Morris (2015); Sabol, Hong, Pianta, & Burchinal (2013). While most QRIS focus on structural quality metrics, some integrate more complex metrics of process quality (e.g., the quality of teaching), especially to achieve higher rating levels.

[63] Bryk et al. (2010); Kraft & Papay (2014); Whalen et al. (2016); Rodd (2012).

intentionally developed to be aligned with an existing measure of school climate—the *5Essentials*—while also attending to the unique experiences inherent in early education settings. The alignment between the ECE and K-12 versions of the surveys provides a common lens, language, and metric for understanding and promoting instructional improvement across the educational continuum. The larger hope is that a common focus on organizational conditions will support the alignment of practices and experiences that children and parents undergo as children transition from preschool to kindergarten.[64]

The use of the *Early Ed Essentials* has the potential to support new areas of research in ECE that can expand our understanding of leadership, teacher and family experiences, and program effectiveness. As the *Early Ed Essentials* surveys are used more broadly in the field, there will be further opportunities to better understand how these constructs are related to characteristics of ECE settings, staff, leaders, students, families, and/or communities. For example, we could ask whether structures, standards, expectations, or program composition may differ across sites with higher or lower scores on the *Early Ed Essentials*. We could also start to better understand *how* leadership influences the other parts of the system (i.e., the other essential supports) to improve student outcomes. For example, Sebastian and colleagues studied the pathways from Effective Leadership to student outcomes and compared how those pathways differed in high schools compared to elementary schools.[65] While there were some common paths (e.g., through teacher leadership), there were also differences; it will be important to understand what those pathways look like within ECE settings so that we, as a field, better understand the leverage points for improvement. The use of the *Early Ed Essentials* can also provide contextual information about programs that may shed light into other long-standing early education research questions, such as why some programs seem to thrive and others do not even when similar structural conditions exist. While we only list several, we believe there are many other research questions that can be informed by the theory and data that emerge from the *Early Ed Essentials*.

Limitations

We acknowledge a number of limitations to the current study, which we hope to address over time. First, it is important to note that all of these relationships are correlational. While some of the existing work in K-12 has shown that school climate and conditions *precede* changes in student outcomes,[66] the current cross-sectional exploration looks at survey responses and site-level outcomes concurrently. As the *Early Ed Essentials* becomes used more widely, future research can start to decipher whether the surveys are simply picking up on factors that are the *results* of having engaged families and positive teacher-child interactions, or whether these organizational conditions set the stage for improvement efforts. Additionally, with more data (and time), we hope to better understand whether organizational conditions can *predict* future improvement in programs. We also look forward to opportunities to look at the relationship between the *Early Ed Essentials* and other outcomes, such as kindergarten readiness.

Most of the development of the *Early Ed Essentials* and all the validation testing has taken place in the city of Chicago. It may be that these surveys function differently in smaller cities, rural, or suburban settings or within different state or local contexts. Early indications are that the psychometric properties do hold across different locations across the country; during the pilot phase of this work, the teacher survey was piloted not only in Chicago

---

64 Kauerz & Coffman (2013).
65 Sebastian, Allensworth, & Huang (2016).
66 e.g., Bryk, et al. (2010).

but also through the national Family and Child Experiences Survey (FACES) study.[67] However, relationships with outcomes, or the range of responses received in response to the surveys may differ.

In addition to being a one-city sample, our validation study sample had a couple other minor limitations. We had a lower teacher survey completion rate in center-based sites compared to schools which is likely due to the differences in survey administration procedures (i.e., school-based data collection through centralized administration of an annual survey for all staff vs. research staff collecting data in community-based sites). We also had lower rates of participation from sites serving predominantly Black children. Future administrations of the *Early Ed Essentials* may want to consider different approaches to encouraging sites to participate and staff and families to complete the survey.

Lastly, these surveys have been tested with a specific sub-group of ECE settings—those that focus on educational outcomes and that have at least three classrooms serving preschool-age students. While this tool may not be appropriate for all early care settings serving children ages 3-5, future work can focus on identifying which aspects of these essential supports are necessary for *any* type of early care setting and begin to expand use into those settings, including settings supported primarily through child care funding and group settings serving infants and toddlers. This is critical, since there are almost 80,000 center-based sites across the country providing early education to children age birth through 5 that do not receive either Head Start or public pre-k funding.[68] As with the current work, careful attention will need to be paid to whether the surveys align with expectations and experiences in those various settings and whether they are related to other established measures of quality.

The current study is only the first in what we intend to be ongoing work aimed at better measuring and understanding organizational conditions essential to best supporting the learning of young children and their families within ECE settings. Findings indicate that the *Early Ed Essentials* surveys are 1) reliable and valid, 2) able to measure differences in the climate and culture experienced by staff and families in different types of ECE settings, and 3) associated with established indicators of ECE program quality and student attendance. This measurement development and testing effort will spur future research, practice, and policy efforts focused on understanding and improving the role of organizational conditions within ECE contexts as a critical lever to increase instructional quality, enhance interactions and relationships between leaders, staff, families, and students, and advance children's outcomes.

---

67 See Ehrlich et al. (2016) for more information.
68 These most current data are from 2012. These center-based sites represent 61 percent of all center-based sites across the country (National Survey of Early Care and Education Project Team, 2015).

References

Allensworth, E., Ponisciak, S., & Mazzeo, C. (2009)
The schools teachers leave: Teacher mobility in Chicago Public Schools. Chicago, IL: Consortium on Chicago School Research.

Aikens, N., Klein, A.K., Tarullo, L., & West, J. (2013)
Getting ready for kindergarten: Children's progress during Head Start. FACES 2009 report (OPRE Report 2013-21a). Washington, DC: Office of Planning, Research & Evaluation, Administration for Children & Families, U.S. Department of Health.

Balfanz, R., & Byrnes, V. (2012)
The importance of being in school: A report on absenteeism in the nation's public schools. Baltimore, MD: Johns Hopkins University Center for Social Organization of Schools.

Barnett, W.S., Friedman-Krauss, A.H., Gomez, R., Horowitz, M., Weisenfeld, G.G., Brown, K. C., & Squires, J.H. (2016)
The state of preschool 2015: State preschool yearbook. New Brunswick, NJ: National Institute for Early Education Research.

Bassock, D., Markowtiz, A.J., Player, D., & Zagardo, M. (2017)
Working paper: Do parents know "high quality" preschool when they see it? Charlottesville, VA: EdPolicyWorks. Retrieved from https://curry.virginia.edu/uploads/resourceLibrary/54_Can_Parents_Assess_Preschool_Quality.pdf

Blair, C., & Razza, R.P. (2007)
Relating effortful control, executive function, and false belief understanding to emerging math and literacy ability in kindergarten. *Child Development, 78*(2), 647-663.

Bloom, P.J. (2010)
Measuring work attitudes in the early childhood setting: Technical manual for the early childhood job satisfaction survey and early childhood work environment survey. Wheeling, IL: McCormick Center for Early Childhood Leadership.

Bryant, D. (2010)
Observational measures of quality in center-based early care and education programs (OPRE Brief No. 2011-10c). Washington, DC: U.S. Department of Health and Human Services, Administration for Children and Families, Office of Planning, Research and Evaluation. Retrieved from http://www.acf.hhs.gov/programs/opre/cc/childcare_technical/reports/observe_measures.Pdf

Bryk, A.S., Sebring, P.B., Allensworth, E., Luppescu, S., & Easton, J.Q. (2010)
Organizing schools for improvement: Lessons from Chicago. Chicago, IL: The University of Chicago Press.

Bryk, A., & Raudenbush, S.W. (1992)
Hierarchical linear models for social and behavioral research: Applications and data analysis methods. Newbury Park, CA: Sage.

The Build Initiative and Child Trends. (2015)
A catalog and comparison of Quality Rating and Improvement Systems (QRIS). Retrieved from http://qriscompendium.org/

Burchinal, M., Vandergrift, N., Pianta, R.C., & Mashburn, A. (2010)
Threshold analysis of association between child care quality and child outcomes for low-income children in prekindergarten programs. *Early Childhood Research Quarterly, 25*(2), 166-176.

Creswell, J.W., & Plano Clark, V.L. (2011)
Designing and conducting mixed methods research (2nd Ed.). Thousand Oaks, CA: Sage.

Clements, D.H., & Sarama, J. (2004)
Learning trajectories in mathematics education. *Mathematical Thinking and Learning, 6*(2), 81-89.

Connolly, F., & Olsen, L.S. (2012)
Early elementary performance and attendance in Baltimore City Schools' pre-kindergarten and kindergarten. Baltimore, MD: Baltimore Education Research Consortium.

Connors, M., & Morris, P. (2015)
Comparing state policy approaches to early care and education quality: A multidimensional assessment of Quality Rating and Improvement Systems and child care licensing regulations. *Early Childhood Research Quarterly, 30*(B), 266-279.

Cook, P., Crowley, M., Dodge, K., & Gearing, M. (2015, November 12)
Primary school truancy: Risk factors and consequences for subsequent dropout. Paper presented at the Association for Public Policy Analysis & Management Annual Fall Research Conference, Miami, FL.

Cunningham, A.E., & Stanovich, K.E. (1997)
Early reading acquisition and its relation to reading experience and ability 10 years later. *Developmental Psychology, 33*(6), 934-945.

Dennis, S.E., & O'Connor, E. (2013)
Reexamining quality in early childhood education: Exploring the relationship between the organizational climate and the classroom. *Journal of Research in Childhood Education, 27*(1), 74-92.

de Winter, J.C., & Dodou, D. (2012)
Factor recovery by principal axis factoring and maximum likelihood factor analysis as a function of factor pattern and sample size. *Journal of Applied Statistics, 39*(4), 695-710.

Dubay, L., & Holla, N. (2015)
Absenteeism in DC Public Schools Early Education Program. Washington, DC: Urban Institute.

Early, D.M., Maxwell, K.L., Burchinal, M., Alva, S., Bender, R.H., Bryant, D., ... & Henry, G.T. (2007)
Teachers' education, classroom quality, and young children's academic skills: Results from seven studies of preschool programs. *Child Development, 78*(2), 558-580.

Ehrlich, S.B., Gwynne, J.A., & Allensworth, E.M. (forthcoming)
Preschool attendance attendance matters: Early chronic absence patterns and relationships to learning outcomes. *Early Childhood Research Quarterly.*

Ehrlich, S.B., Gwynne, J.A., Pareja, A.S., & Allensworth, E.M. (2014)
Preschool attendance in Chicago Public Schools: Relationship with learning outcomes and reasons for absences. Chicago, IL: University of Chicago Consortium on Chicago School Research.

Ehrlich, S.B., Pacchiano, D.M., Stein, A.G., & Luppescu, S. (2016)
Essential organizational supports for early education: The development of a new survey tool to measure organizational conditions. Chicago, IL: University of Chicago Consortium on School Research and Ounce of Prevention Fund.

Fabrigar, L.R., & Wegener, D.T. (2011)
Exploratory factor analysis. New York, NY: Oxford University Press.

Feldt, L.S., & Qualls, A.L. (1999)
Variability in reliability coefficients and the standard error of measurement from school district to district. *Applied Measurement in Education, 12*(4), 367-381.

Fixsen, D.L., Naoom, S.F., Blase, K.A., & Friedman, R.M. (2005)
Implementation research: a synthesis of the literature. Tampa, FL: University of South Florida, Louis de la Parte Florida Mental Health Institute, The National Implementation Research Network.

Howes, C., Burchinal, M., Pianta, R., Bryant, D., Early, D., Clifford, R., & Barbarin, O. (2008)
Ready to learn? Children's pre-academic achievement in pre-kindergarten programs. *Early Childhood Research Quarterly, 23*(1), 27-50.

Hu, B.Y., Zhou, Y., & Li, K. (2017)
Variations in Chinese parental perceptions of early childhood education quality. *European Early Childhood Education Research Journal, 25*(4), 519-540.

Kauerz, K., & Coffman, J. (2013)
Framework for planning, implementing, and evaluating preK-3rd grade approaches. Seattle, WA: College of Education, University of Washington.

Kim, D.H., Lambert, R.G., & Burts, D.C. (2013)
Evidence of the validity of Teaching Strategies GOLD® assessment tool for English language learners and children with disabilities. *Early Education & Development, 24*(4), 574-595.

Kim, D.H., Lambert, R.G., & Burts, D.C. (2014)
Validating a developmental scale for young children using the Rasch model: Applicability of the teaching strategies GOLD assessment system. *Journal of Applied Measurement, 15*(4), 405-421.

Kraft, M.A., Marinell, W.H., & Shen-Wei Yee, D. (2016)
School organizational contexts, teacher turnover, and student achievement: Evidence from panel data. *American Educational Research Journal, 53*(5), 1411-1449.

Kraft, M.A., & Papay, J.P. (2014)
Can professional environments in schools promote teacher development? Explaining heterogeneity in returns to teaching experience. *Educational Evaluation and Policy Analysis, 36*(4), 476-500.

Lambert, R.G., Kim, D.H., Taylor, H., & McGee, J.R. (2010)
Technical manual for the Teaching Strategies GOLD® assessment system. Charlotte, NC: Center for Educational Measurement and Evaluation.

Linacre, J.M. (2015)
A user's guide to Winsteps (program manual 3.91.0). Retrieved from http://www.winsteps.com/manuals.htm

Liu, X., Spybrook, J., Congdon, R., Martinez, A., & Raudenbush, S. (2005)
Optimal design for multi-level and longitudinal research. Ann Arbor, MI: Survey Research Center of the Institute of Social Research at the University of Michigan.

Lower, J.K. & Cassidy, D.J. (2007)
Child care work environments: The relationship with learning environments. *Journal of Research in Childhood Education, 22*(2), 189-204.

Mashburn, A.J., Pianta, R.C., Hamre, B.K., Downer, J.T., Barbarin, O.A., Bryant, D., ... & Howes, C. (2008)
Measures of classroom quality in prekindergarten and children's development of academic, language, and social skills. *Child Development, 79*(3), 732-749.

McClelland, M.M., Morrison, F.J., & Holmes, D.L. (2000)
Children at risk for early academic problems: The role of learning-related social skills. *Early Childhood Research Quarterly, 15*(3), 307-329.

Meyers, M.K., & Jordan, L.P. (2006)
Choice and accommodation in parent child care decisions. *Community Development, 37*(2), 53-70.

Miller-Bains, K.L., Russo, J.M., Williford, A.P., DeCoster, J., & Cottone, E.A. (2017)
Examining the validity of a multidimensional performance-based assessment at kindergarten entry. *AERA Open, 3*(2), 1-16.

National Early Literacy Panel. (2008)
Developing early literacy: Report of the National Early Literacy Panel. Washington, DC: National Institute for Literacy.

National Survey of Early Care and Education Project Team (2015)
Which early care and education centers participate in Head Start or public pre-kindergarten? OPRE Report #2015-92a. Washington DC: Office of Planning, Research and Evaluation, Administration for Children and Families, U.S. Department of Health and Human Services. Retrieved from http://www.acf.hhs.gov/programs/opre/research/project/national-survey-of-early-care-and-education-nsece-2010-2014

Nauer, K., White, A., & Yerneni, R. (2008)
Strengthening school by strengthening families. Community strategies to reverse chronic absenteeism in the early grade and improve supports for children and families. New York, NY: The New School.

Nunnally, J.C. (1978)
Psychometric Theory (2nd Ed.). New York, NY: McGraw-Hill.

Office of Head Start, Administration for Children and Families. (2013)
2013 Head Start grantee-level data from the Classroom Assessment Scoring System (CLASS®). Washington, DC: Office of Head Start. Retrieved from https://eclkc.ohs.acf.hhs.gov/sites/default/files/pdf/national-class-2013-data.pdf

Office of Head Start, Administration for Children and Families. (2014)
2014 Head Start grantee-level data from the Classroom Assessment Scoring System (CLASS®). Washington, DC: Office of Head Start. Retrieved from https://eclkc.ohs.acf.hhs.gov/sites/default/files/pdf/national-class-2014-data.pdf

Office of Head Start, Administration for Children and Families. (2015)
2015 Head Start grantee-level data from the Classroom Assessment Scoring System (CLASS®). Washington, DC: Office of Head Start. Retrieved from https://eclkc.ohs.acf.hhs.gov/sites/default/files/pdf/national-class-2015-data.pdf

Osborne, J.W. & Banjanovic, E.S. (2016)
Exploratory Factor Analysis with SAS. Cary, NC: SAS Institute Inc.

Palinkas, L.A., Horwitz, S.M., Green, C.A., Wisdom, J.P., Duan, N., & Hoagwood, K. (2015)
Purposeful sampling for qualitative data collection and analysis in mixed method implementation research. *Administration and Policy in Mental Health and Mental Health Services Research, 42*(5), 533-544.

Pallas, A.M., & Buckley, C.K. (2012)
Thoughts of leaving: An exploration of why New York City middle school teachers consider leaving their classrooms. New York, NY: Research Alliance for New York City Schools.

Park, M., O'Toole, A., & Katsiaficas, C. (2017)
Dual language learners: A national demographic and policy profile. Washington, DC: Migration Policy Institute. Retrieved from https://www.migrationpolicy.org/research/dual-language-learners-national-demographic-and-policy-profile

Park, Y.S. (2017)
Validity studies of the GOLD Assessment System. Unpublished manuscript. Chicago, IL: University of Chicago Consortium on School Research.

Pianta, R.C., La Paro, K.M., & Hamre, B.K. (2008)
Classroom Assessment Scoring System (CLASS). Baltimore, MD: Paul H. Brookes Publishing Co.

Rodd, J. (2012)
Leadership in early childhood. London, UK: McGraw-Hill Education.

Rohacek, M. Adams, G.C., Kisker, E.E., Danziger, A., Derrick-Mills, T., & Johnson, H. (2010)
Understanding quality in context: Child care centers, communities, markets, and public policy. Washington, DC: Urban Institute. Retrieved from https://www.urban.org/sites/default/files/publication/29051/412191-Understanding-Quality-in-Context-Child-Care-Centers-Communities-Markets-and-Public-Policy.PDF

Romero, M., & Lee, Y. (2007)
A national portrait of chronic absenteeism in the early grades. New York, NY: National Center for Children in Poverty, Columbia University.

Sabol, T.J., Hong, S.S., Pianta, R.C., & Burchinal, M.R. (2013)
Can rating pre-K programs predict children's learning? *Science, 341*(6148), 845-846.

Sebastian, J., Allensworth, E., & Huang, H. (2016)
The role of teacher leadership in how principals influence classroom instruction and student learning. *American Journal of Education, 123*(1), 69-108.

Valentino, R. (2017)
Will public pre-K really close achievement gaps? Gaps in prekindergarten quality between students and across states. *American Educational Research Journal.* Advance online publication. https://doi.org/10.3102/0002831217732000

Whalen, S. P., Horsley, H. L., Parkinson, K. K., & Pacchiano, D. (2016)
A development evaluation study of a professional development initiative to strengthen organizational conditions in early education settings. *Journal of Applied Research on Children: Informing Policy for Children at Risk, 7*(2), Article 9.

Wright, B.D., & Masters, G.N. (1982)
Rating scale analysis: Rasch measurement. Chicago, IL: MESA Press.

Zaslow, M., Tout, K., & Martinez-Beck, I. (2010)
Measuring the Quality of Early Care and Education Programs at the Intersection of Research, Policy, and Practice (OPRE Research-to-Policy, Research-to-Practice Brief OPRE 2011-10a). Washington, DC: Office of Planning, Research and Evaluation, Administration for Children and Families, U.S. Department of Health and Human Services.

Appendix
Additional Tables

TABLE A.1
Teacher Survey Measure Characteristics

Measure	# Items in Measure	Rasch Person Reliability[a]	# Items with Significant & Large DIFs by Agency	ICC	School Reliability
Reflective Dialogue	6	0.83	0	0.167	0.538
Socialization of New Teachers	3	0.82	2	0.177	0.557
Teacher Collaboration	5	0.84	0	0.200	0.536
Data Use	5	0.83	0	0.225	0.523
Collective Responsibility	5	0.92	2	0.115	0.471
Innovation	4	0.92	0	0.124	0.490
School Commitment	4	0.73	4	0.245	0.664
Teacher Safety	6	0.83	1	0.517	0.831
Teacher-Principal/Director Trust	8	0.92	1	0.194	0.610
Teacher-Teacher Trust	5	0.87	2	0.131	0.499
Teacher-Parent Trust	5	0.91	1	0.144	0.475
Parent Involvement	4	0.89	0	0.261	0.628
Teacher Outreach/Collaboration with Parents*	7	0.83	1	0.082	0.348
Parent Influence	5	0.87	2	0.127	0.481
Instructional Leadership	7	0.85	2	0.223	0.647
Teacher Influence	5	0.90	0	0.193	0.597
Program Coherence	5	0.79	0	0.209	0.561
Quality of Student Interaction*	4	0.84	1	0.045	0.192
Positive Learning Climate*	6	0.83	0	0.032	0.144
Child-Child Interactions*	4	0.80	0	0.071	0.275
Early Mathematics Development*	4	0.83	1	0.060	0.246
Early Language and Literacy*	5	0.83	0	0.029	0.132
Early Cognitive Development*	4	0.80	0	0.036	0.167
Early Social-Emotional Development*	5	0.82	0	0.025	0.121

Notes: [a] Rasch person reliabilities were obtained from table 3.1 in Winsteps output. ICCs and school reliabilities were obtained from our 3-level measurement HLM models nesting person measure scores within sites, adjusting for person error at level 1.

* New measure created for *Early Ed Essentials* and not included in K-12 *5Essentials*.

TABLE A.2

Parent Survey Measure Characteristics

Measure	# Items in Measure	Rasch Person Reliability[a]	# Items with Significant & Large DIFs by Agency	# Items with Significant & Large DIFs by Language	ICC	School Reliability
Support for Kindergarten Transition	6	0.81	0	1	0.051	0.403
Principal/Director-Parent Relationships	6	0.87	0	0	0.117	0.728
Program Orientation towards Early Education	4	0.84	0	0	0.025	0.332
Staff Care of Parent as Person	4	0.89	0	0	0.045	0.517
Including Parents as Partners	6	0.80	0	2	0.034	0.407
Teacher Communication with Parents	4	0.89	0	1	0.043	0.491
Teachers' Interactions with Children	4	0.93	0	0	0.022	0.355
Parent Influence on the Program	4	0.89	0	0	0.038	0.469
Social-Capital Building of Parents	4	0.87	0	1	0.072	0.620

Notes: [a] Rasch person reliabilities were obtained from table 3.1 in Winsteps output. ICCs and school reliabilities were obtained from our 3-level measurement HLM models nesting person measure scores within sites, adjusting for person error at level 1. All measures were newly created for testing of the *Early Ed Essentials* survey.

TABLE A.3

Loadings from Exploratory Factor Analysis on Teacher and Parent Survey Measures

	Factor 1	Factor 2	Factor 3	Factor 4	Factor 5
Instructional Leadership	0.89				
Teacher-Principal Trust	0.80				
Innovation	0.87				
Collective Responsibility	0.80				
Socialization of New Teachers	0.83				
School Commitment	0.78				
Teacher Influence	0.83				0.61
Program Coherence	0.76				
Teacher-Teacher Trust	0.70				
Teacher Collaboration	0.78				
Parent Influence	0.74				0.52
Staff Care of Parent as Person (P)		0.85			
Teacher Communication (P)		0.83			
Including Parents as Partners (P)		0.80			
Parent Social Capital Building (P)		0.80			
Parent Influence on the Program (P)		0.68			
Support for Kindergarten Transition (P)		0.67			
Principal-Parent Relationships (P)		0.65			
Orientation to Education (P)		0.63			
Early Literacy and Language			0.80		
Early Math			0.82		
Early Cognitive Development			0.80		
Early Social-Emotional			0.72		
Positive Learning Climate			0.73		
Quality of Student Interactions			0.64		
Child-Child Interactions			0.60		0.56
Teacher Outreach with Parents			0.53		
Teacher Safety				0.59	
Reflective Dialogue	0.63				0.61
Collective Use of Assessment Data	0.62			-0.54	
Teachers Interactions with Children (P)					0.61
Teacher-Parent Trust	0.65				0.76
Parent Involvement	0.55		0.55		0.69

Notes: (P) = Parent Survey. Factors were extracted using principal axis factoring and oblique rotation. Loadings represent the product-moment correlations between the variables and common factors. Table shows loadings > |+/-0.50|.

TABLE A.4

HLM Coefficients Relating Essential Scores to CLASS Scores, using Subsamples of Sites Satisfying Response Rate Criteria

	Emotional Support				Classroom Organization				Instructional Support			
	Unadjusted		Adjusted		Unadjusted		Adjusted		Unadjusted		Adjusted	
	CoE	P-Val	CoE	P-Val	CoE	P-Val	CoE	P-Val	CoE	P-Val	CoE	P-Val
Effective Instructional Leaders	0.124	0.165	0.107	0.241	0.196	0.047	0.167	0.085	0.184	0.045	0.167	0.063
Collaborative Teachers	0.193	0.027	0.173	0.056	0.277	0.004	0.237	0.013	0.251	0.005	0.238	0.007
Ambitious Instruction	-0.169	0.049	-0.185	0.037	-0.118	0.223	-0.152	0.115	-0.150	0.092	-0.147	0.101
Supportive Environment	0.014	0.883	-0.048	0.660	0.098	0.337	0.020	0.866	0.048	0.614	0.011	0.920
Involved Families	0.014	0.875	-0.008	0.934	0.036	0.728	0.002	0.985	0.059	0.533	0.021	0.821
Parent Voice	-0.015	0.880	-0.010	0.917	0.051	0.627	0.051	0.609	0.075	0.417	0.065	0.466

CoE = Coefficient; P-Val = P-Value

Note: Each essential coefficient comes from a separate model in which only that essential was included as a predictor. Coefficients are presented in standardized terms. Unadjusted models do not include covariates; adjusted models control for racial composition (integrated, predominantly Latino, predominantly Black, or racially mixed) and share of students whose primary language is not English. For essentials based on teacher survey measures (i.e., Effective Instructional Leaders, Collaborative Teachers, Ambitious Instruction, Supportive Environment, Involved Families), models were fit using 53 sites that meet criteria for teacher survey response rate and CLASS score report rate; for Parent Voice, models were fit using 52 sites that meet criteria for parent survey response rate and CLASS score report rate. The CLASS was standardized at the classroom level (within each domain) and then entered into the models.

TABLE A.5

HLM Coefficients Relating Essential Scores to Student Attendance Rates, using Subsamples of Sites Satisfying Response Rate Criteria

	Unadjusted		Adjusted	
	Coefficient	P-Value	Coefficient	P-Value
Effective Instructional Leaders	2.297	0.002	1.649	0.011
Collaborative Teachers	2.717	0.000	1.889	0.003
Ambitious Instruction	0.927	0.214	0.405	0.538
Supportive Environment	2.476	0.001	1.244	0.099
Involved Families	1.990	0.009	1.360	0.040
Parent Voice	1.115	0.190	0.829	0.224

Note: Each essential coefficient comes from a separate model in which only that essential was included as a predictor. Unadjusted models do not include covariates; adjusted model controls for racial composition (integrated, predominantly Latino, predominantly Black, or racially mixed), share of students whose primary language is not English, and share of three-year-old students. For essentials based on teacher survey measures (i.e., Effective Instructional Leaders, Collaborative Teachers, Ambitious Instruction, Supportive Environment, Involved Families), models were fit using 68 sites that meet criteria for teacher survey response rate; for Parent Voice, models were fit using 74 sites that meet criteria for parent survey response rate. Student attendance was entered into the models in percentage values (e.g., 90 percent entered as 90).

ABOUT THE AUTHORS

STACY B. EHRLICH is a Senior Research Scientist at NORC at the University of Chicago. She was a Managing Director and Senior Research Scientist at the UChicago Consortium at the time this research was conducted. Ehrlich's research interests include using quantitative methods to measure student learning and growth for the improvement of education. Her work focuses on a range of topics affecting students in Chicago including studying early chronic absenteeism; developing a deeper understanding of how noncognitive factors develop over childhood and adolescence across a variety of contexts; and developing and testing surveys that capture the strengths of organizational supports and structures for effective teaching and learning in early education settings. Ehrlich is also involved in outreach with other research organizations that are implementing research-practitioner partnership models. She holds a PhD in developmental psychology from the University of Chicago and a BS in human development and family studies from the University of Wisconsin-Madison.

DEBRA M. PACCHIANO is Vice President, Translational Research at the Ounce of Prevention Fund. She is responsible for the conceptualization, implementation, and evaluation of applied research initiatives to advance professional learning, quality improvement, and practice innovation in early education teaching, learning, and leadership. Pacchiano recently completed directing a federal Investing in Innovation (i3) grant to design and evaluate a professional development model that strengthens instructional leadership and job-embedded professional learning supports essential to the continuous improvement of teaching and learning in early education settings. Currently, she is providing conceptual, implementation, and evaluation leadership as the Ounce scales this professional development model across the state of Illinois and nationally. Pacchiano holds a PhD from Indiana University in educational psychology with emphasis in school psychology and early childhood special education and a BS in psychology and public policy from the University of Minnesota.

AMANDA G. STEIN is Director, Research and Evaluation at the Ounce of Prevention Fund. Her research interests include studying the short- and long-term trajectories of children and families participating in early education settings and advancing the definition, measurement, and testing of "high-quality" practices and organizational conditions in the early childhood field. Stein directs the Educare Chicago Implementation and Longitudinal Follow-Up Studies and provides research and evaluation leadership on various Ounce initiatives. She has considerable experience partnering with external organizations, including participating in a network of over 20 early childhood researchers conducting secondary data analyses; collaborating with the Erikson Institute on an early math evaluation; and co-leading the evaluation and dissemination for the Birth-To-College Collaborative with the UChicago Urban Education Institute. She was a post-doctoral fellow in early childhood special education policy & leadership at the University of Colorado, and holds a PhD in human development and family studies from Iowa State University and a BS in developmental psychology from Creighton University.

MAUREEN R. WAGNER serves as the Project Manager and provides qualitative research support on the *Early Ed Essentials* project. She also staffs research and policy committees, and supports the work to translate the *Early Ed Essentials* framework to policy solutions. Wagner has cross-sector experience in research, policy, and practice. Prior to working at the Ounce, she designed program evaluation plans for disability service programs at the Minnesota Department of Human Services and facilitated the launch of Minnesota's Own Your Future long-term care planning initiative. She is also a former middle school science and social studies teacher. In addition to her work at the Ounce, Wagner is an active community organizer with Illinois for Education Equity (ILEE) in Chicago. She earned an MPP and an MSW from the University of Minnesota, and a BA in psychology from Illinois State University.

This report reflects the interpretation of the authors. Although the UChicago Consortium's Steering Committee provided technical advice, no formal endorsement by these individuals, organizations, or the full UChicago Consortium should be assumed.

Acknowledgements

We would like to acknowledge the many people who made this work possible and who contributed to this work through their partnership, feedback, support, and encouragement. This work is the result of a strong collaboration between the Ounce of Prevention Fund (Ounce) and the University of Chicago Consortium on School Research (UChicago Consortium). We gratefully acknowledge several funders for their generous support of this work, including an anonymous funder, the Bill & Melinda Gates Foundation, the Joyce Foundation, the W.K. Kellogg Foundation, and the Pritzker Children's Initiative. We also express our deep gratitude to the school principals and community-based center directors who invited us into their programs, as well as the early education preschool teachers, staff, and parents who completed our surveys. A special thank you to the leaders, staff, and families at the four sites that participated in the qualitative study.

Throughout this work, we received active support from the Office of Early Childhood Education at Chicago Public Schools (CPS) and the City of Chicago Department of Family & Support Services (DFSS). Leaders in both agencies have seen the vision for this work, provided critical feedback along the way, and encouraged early education leaders, schools, and community-based centers to participate in our validation study. In particular, we would like to thank Diego Geraldo, Leslie McKinley, Serah Fatani, and Beth Mascitti-Miller from CPS; Beth Stover and the late Vanessa Rich from DFSS, and Samantha Aigner-Treworgy from the City of Chicago Mayor's Office.

We also benefited from the ongoing feedback and support of our colleagues at the UChicago Consortium and the Ounce. We want to thank Penny Bender Sebring, Tony Raden, and Ann Hanson for being part of our larger project team and providing critical insights on this work. They helped ensure we were continuously attending to the broader needs of the early education practice and policy communities. We also had an outstanding advisory committee, comprised of Elaine Allensworth (UChicago Consortium), Tony Bryk (Carnegie Foundation), Rachel Gordon (University of Illinois-Chicago), Karen Mapp (Harvard University), Robert Pianta (University of Virginia), and Diana Rauner (Ounce), who greatly shaped the content of the surveys and the design of the validation study. Our special thanks also goes out to Elliot Ransom at the University of Chicago Impact for his insights on survey adoption, implementation, use, and scaling, as well as Molly Gordon (UChicago Consortium) for providing guidance and review on the qualitative study.

A number of colleagues affiliated with UChicago Consortium, the Ounce, and their collaborating organizations served as readers and thought partners as we conceptualized, analyzed, and wrote many drafts of this technical report and accompanying snapshot. In particular, we would like to thank Gina Caneva, Maia Connors, Holly Hart, Marsha Hawley, Kylie Klein, Rebecca Klein, Eleni Manos, Louisiana Meléndez, Sara Nadig, and Rebecca Vonderlack-Navarro for their very close reads of drafts of this technical report. We thank our communications staff, Bronwyn McDaniel, Jessica Puller, R. Steven Quispe, and Jessica Tansey from UChicago Consortium and Jason Sommer from the Ounce, for their insightful feedback, careful readings, and support for production and dissemination.

This project would not be possible without the help of our project manager, research assistants, and teams of data collectors. We especially thank Nicholas Walker-Craig for supporting the development of surveys and analyses, and assisting with site recruitment; our lead data collectors Beth Frank, Nathalie Tirado Gonzalez, and Claudia Melgar who persisted tirelessly with recruitment and leading teams of data collectors into the field; and Ruby Garrett who made countless recruitment calls and visits to invite sites to participate in our study.

We appreciate the support from the Consortium Investor Council, which funds critical work beyond the initial research: putting the research to work, refreshing the data archive, seeding new studies, and replicating previous studies. Members include: Brinson Family Foundation, CME Group Foundation, Crown Family Philanthropies, Lloyd A. Fry Foundation, Joyce Foundation, Lewis-Sebring Family Foundation, McCormick Foundation, McDougal Family Foundation, Osa Family Foundation, Polk Bros. Foundation, Spencer Foundation, Steans Family Foundation, and The Chicago Public Education Fund. We also gratefully acknowledge the Spencer Foundation and the Lewis-Sebring Family Foundation, whose operating grants support the work of the UChicago Consortium.

This report was produced by the UChicago Consortium's publications and communications staff: Bronwyn McDaniel, Director of Outreach and Communication; Jessica Tansey, Communications Manager; Jessica Puller, Communications Specialist; and R. Steven Quispe, Development and Communications Coordinator.

Graphic Design: Jeff Hall Design and R. Steven Quispe
Photography: Eileen Ryan
Editing: Jessica Puller and Jessica Tansey

03.2018/pdf/jh.design@rcn.com

UCHICAGO Consortium
on School Research

1313 East 60th Street
Chicago, Illinois 60637
T 773.702.3364
F 773.702.2010

@UChiConsortium
consortium.uchicago.edu

Directors

ELAINE M. ALLENSWORTH
Lewis-Sebring Director

CAMILLE A. FARRINGTON
Managing Director and Senior Research Associate

JULIA A. GWYNNE
Managing Director and Senior Research Scientist

HOLLY HART
Survey Director

KYLIE KLEIN
Director of Research Operations

BRONWYN MCDANIEL
Director of Outreach and Communication

JENNY NAGAOKA
Deputy Director

MELISSA RODERICK
*Senior Director
Hermon Dunlap Smith Professor
School of Social Service Administration*

PENNY BENDER SEBRING
Co-Founder

MARISA DE LA TORRE
Managing Director and Senior Research Associate

Steering Committee

RAQUEL FARMER-HINTON
Co-Chair
University of Wisconsin, Milwaukee

DENNIS LACEWELL
Co-Chair
Urban Prep Charter Academy for Young Men

Ex-Officio Members

SARA RAY STOELINGA
Urban Education Institute

Institutional Members

SARAH DICKSON
Chicago Public Schools

ELIZABETH KIRBY
Chicago Public Schools

TROY LARAVIERE
Chicago Principals and Administrators Association

KAREN G.J. LEWIS
Chicago Teachers Union

ALAN MATHER
Chicago Public Schools

TONY SMITH
Illinois State Board of Education

Individual Members

GINA CANEVA
Lindblom Math & Science

NANCY CHAVEZ
OneGoal

KATIE HILL
Office of the Cook County State's Attorney

MEGAN HOUGARD
Chicago Public Schools

GREG JONES
Kenwood Academy

PRANAV KOTHARI
Revolution Impact, LLC

LILA LEFF
Umoja Student Development Corporation & Emerson Collective

RITO MARTINEZ
Surge Institute

LUISIANA MELÉNDEZ
Erikson Institute

SHAZIA MILLER
NORC at the University of Chicago

CRISTINA PACIONE-ZAYAS
Erikson Institute

BEATRIZ PONCE DE LEÓN
Generation All

PAIGE PONDER
One Million Degrees

KATHLEEN ST. LOUIS CALIENTO
The Academy Group

AMY TREADWELL
Chicago New Teacher Center

REBECCA VONDERLACK-NAVARRO
Latino Policy Forum

PAM WITMER
Illinois Network of Charter Schools

JOHN ZEIGLER
DePaul University

www.ingramcontent.com/pod-product-compliance
Lightning Source LLC
Chambersburg PA
CBHW042007100426
42738CB00039B/54